BEYOND

THE SHADOWS

Discover Hope for Overcoming

DEPRESSION

PICKINGUP
THEPIECES

BY RAMON PRESSON WITH BEN COLTER

Beyond the Shadows: Discover Hope for Overcoming Depression
© 2008 Serendipity House

Published by Serendipity House Publishers
Nashville, Tennessee

ISBN: 978-1-5749-4351-1
Item Number: 005038476

To purchase additional copies of this resource or other studies:
ORDER ONLINE at www.SerendipityHouse.com;
WRITE Serendipity House, 117 10th Avenue North, Nashville, TN 37234
FAX (615) 277-8181
PHONE (800) 458-2772

1-800-458-2772
www.SerendipityHouse.com

Printed in the United States of America
14 13 12 11 10 09 08   1 2 3 4 5 6 7 8 9 10

CONTENTS

Picking Up the Pieces Resources

Real help for real people living real life.

How do we make sense of the times of pain and suffering in our lives? How can we reconcile the reality of our pain with the goodness of God?

Whenever you struggle, God's heart aches for you. He desperately wants to walk with you through the difficult and desperate times of your life so He can lead you to hope, healing, and freedom. Picking Up the Pieces is a series of honest, experiential Bible studies that will help you along the unfamiliar journey of rediscovering your heart!

- Written by leading therapists from the American Association of Christian Counselors
- Honest, experiential Bible studies that will set captives free from destructive patterns
- Probing questions for your heart and for God to help bind up the broken places
- Unique journaling experiences at the end of each session
- Replaces beauty for ashes and glory for shame

GREAT RESOURCES FOR:

- Support Groups
- Small Groups
- Accountability Groups

- Recovery Groups
- Church Classes and Soul Care Ministries
- Counseling Centers

BEYOND THE SHADOWS
DISCOVER HOPE FOR OVERCOMING DEPRESSION

None of us walks through this life unscathed. At some point we all experience what Saint John of the Cross referred to as "the dark night of the soul." Sometimes it feels like our happiness has been stolen and our enthusiasm ripped off by some thieving intruder. Our delight with life seems to have evaporated like a mist, and we wonder if we'll ever see it again. Depression affects every dimension of our lives: physical, emotional, spiritual, and relational. Left unchecked, it can overwhelm us and devastate our lives.

An eight-session, small-group experience is not likely to "cure" someone suffering with depression. Instant cures and quick temporary fixes are not what *Beyond the Shadows* offers. But you can discover hope, a healthy way to respond to depression, and a path for overcoming the devastating effects of depression.

As we explore a deeper understanding of depression and its physical, emotional, social, and spiritual impacts, you'll be encouraged to break through to better emotional balance and happiness. We can accept the reality of depression without just giving into it. In eight group sessions we'll explore better ways of coping and discuss how to push back against depression. After all, depression is a bully, and bullies have to be resisted and given a shove in return now and then.

Beyond the Shadows is a unique experiential resource designed to walk you through the experiences, feelings, and struggles that are common to depression. This study will help group members to be real about their hurts and fears. It will also guide you to track down and capture your joy thieves so you can recover reasons to smile and excuses to laugh. Best of all, you'll join with others on the journey to find that healing occurs best within a caring community.

REFILLING OUR TANKS

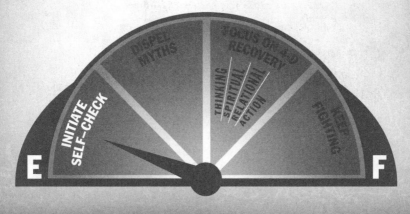

King David, a one the Bible calls, "a man after God's own heart" knew well how it feels to be in the shadows of depression. Psalm 69 captures the lament of his soul.

Paraphrase of Psalm 69

<u>neck.</u>

Save me, O God, for the waters are up to my

I

s

i

n

k   in the miry depths

where there is no foothold,

nothing solid, reliable.

I am worn out calling for **HELP !**

My throat hurts and my voice is gone.

My eyes are tired and bloodshot from

looking, staring, searching for you.

WHERE ARE YOU?

I call out to you with my last breaths.

Rescue me from this quicksand;

I feel I'm about to go

<u>under.</u>

Shades of Gray:
The Spectrum of Depression

Breaking the Ice - 15-20 minutes

> LEADER: *Be sure to read the introductory pages in the front of the book as well as the leader's notes in the back. "Breaking the Ice" is designed to put group members at ease and to get them talking. Choose whether your group will respond to question 2a or 2b. For question 2a, you will need to secure a box of 64 Crayola® crayons in advance.*

1. Take turns introducing yourselves to the group. Share your name, one thing about yourself that your friends would say is unusual or unique, and finally one reason you joined this group.

2a. As you pass around a box of 64 Crayolas,® each of you will select a favorite color and identify what (an object, a quality, an experience, a memory, a special location or person) you associate with your color.

2b. Even though we use phrases like "singing the blues," many people associate depression with the color gray. What do you think it is about gray that makes it the "color" of depression? If you prefer another color to represent depression, what is it?

3. Look at the picture of the children in the tree illustration. With which child do you most identify, or which one best identifies your current emotional state? Discuss your responses as a group.

Opening Prayer

God, join us as we begin this journey together. Sometimes it feels as though our joy has been misplaced like a set of keys, or dropped and shattered like a fragile vase. Sometimes it feels like our happiness has been stolen—our enthusiasm ripped off by some thieving intruder. Our delight with life seems to have disappeared and we wonder if we'll ever see it again. Lord, help us to be real with You and with each other about our hurt and our fears. Help us lean into our pain without falling over the rail. Help us track down and capture the joy thieves and recover reasons to smile and excuses to laugh.

Objectives for this Session

- Understand the symptoms of depression
- Recognize the current level of my depression
- Identify healthy vs. unhealthy strategies for coping
- Utilize a measurement of improvement
- Prepare to begin a healthy journey of responding to depression with the aid of a supportive group

Discovering the Truth – 35-40 Minutes

You're Not Alone

According to the World Health Organization, more than 121 million people suffer from depression. It's among the leading causes for disability worldwide. The National Institute for Mental Health reports that more than 19 million people in the U.S. suffer from depression; that's nearly 10% of the U.S. population. Depression is often linked with anxiety disorder, panic disorder, and substance abuse.

1. Are you surprised by the statistics on depression? How do these numbers affect your feelings about dealing with your own depression?

Even spiritual giants suffer from occasional depression. At times the symptoms and feelings can be rather severe. Many men and women of faith have felt a heaviness of heart, and some have afflicted by profound seasons of melancholy. You are not alone!

After an impressive display of Elijah's faith and courage, complete with taunting the opposition, the Lord sent fire down from heaven onto Mount Carmel and consumed the sacrifice that the pagan Baal worshipers were unable to ignite (1 Kings 18). The humiliated prophets of Baal were slaughtered in the Kishon Valley. Despite this overwhelming victory, one powerful woman by means of a death threat sent Elijah fleeing more than 100 miles to hide out at Beer-sheba.

³ Then Elijah became afraid and immediately ran for his life. When he came to Beer-sheba that belonged to Judah, he left his servant there, ⁴ but he went on a day's journey into the wilderness. He sat down under a broom tree and prayed that he might die. He said, "I have had enough! LORD, take my life, for I'm no better than my fathers." ⁵ Then he lay down and slept under the broom tree. Suddenly, an angel touched him. The angel told him, "Get up and eat."

1 Kings 19:3-5, HCSB

2. According to 1 Kings 19:3-5, what emotions overcame Elijah following his mountain-top experience? How do you suppose Elijah's emotions could collapse so rapidly?

3. While Elijah did not plan to kill himself, he prayed to die. What do you suppose he wanted God to realize about his feelings?

4. Imagine for a moment that you are Elijah's counselor. You need to explain Elijah's situation to his concerned family. What would you tell them?

RUNNING ON EMPTY

Jackson Browne released the multi-platinum hit song "Running on Empty" in 1977. Those of us struggling with depression can relate to the chorus: *Running on – running on empty. Running on – running blind. Running on – running into the sun, but I'm running behind.* Depression has us running on empty in every area of our lives, but there's hope and healing if we stay in the race. This diagram summarizes the healing journey this group will take together to refill our tanks. This week we begin with initiating a self-check.

REFILLING OUR TANKS

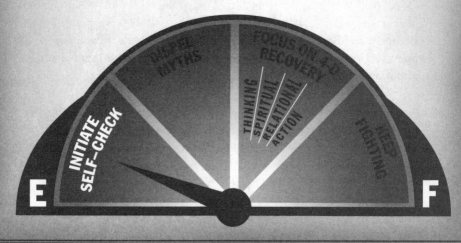

CAUSES OF DEPRESSION

Depression is a complex problem. When trying to trace the root causes of depression we're faced with multiple potential factors. For the most part, these contributing factors fall into two categories: **Situational** and **Physical**.

(1) SITUATIONAL FACTORS

Depression frequently has a situational trigger. Our despairing feelings can be an emotional and spiritual response to some painful or stressful life event.

5. Which of the following situational factors can you relate to as a current or past trigger for depression? Check all that apply and briefly share how one of the situations affected you.

❐ Death or serious illness of someone we love
❐ Divorce, broken engagement, break-up of a dating relationship
❐ Moving away from a familiar community
❐ Spiritual issues or detachment from God
❐ Stress at work, home, or in relationships
❐ A deeply felt failure or loss
❐ Something hoped for that didn't materialize
❐ Family turmoil   ❐ Job loss or problems at work
❐ A personal health crisis   ❐ Financial problems
❐ Rejection or disapproval   ❐ Fear of the future
❐ Other: _____

(2) PHYSICAL FACTORS

Depression is often more than a set of feelings. Depression may have its roots in physiological factors. If you suffer from depression, you should have a thorough examination by your family doctor, and perhaps also by a psychiatric specialist, so you'll know if there are physical factors involved. Some of the more common physical contributors to depression (and there are many others) include:

❐ Chemical imbalances (serotonin, norepinephrine, and/or dopamine)
❐ Hormonal imbalance (estrogen, progesterone, testosterone, or thyroid)
❐ Exhaustion
❐ Insomnia
❐ Long-term conditions such as Diabetes, Multiple Sclerosis, or Cancer
❐ Chronic illness, pain, or fatigue
❐ Blood disorders (low blood pressure or anemia)
❐ Sexually transmitted diseases
❐ Congestive heart failure or pulmonary disorders
❐ Digestive disorders
❐ Some allergies

6. What situational and physical factors do you think might have contributed to Elijah's sudden depression?

7. Look again at the list of physical factors. Do any of these apply to you? (You will not be asked to share your responses, but you are welcome to share if you'd like.)

A few of the physical factors may directly cause depression through an imbalance or malfunction. Others are physical ailments that can provoke or agitate depression—a rather unwanted two-for-one special. These physical factors function much as situational factors do. Loss of health or the ability to function as before can prove depressing.

IMPORTANT NOTE: This group is not equipped to address the physical factors in depression, except to support members as they seek treatment from their physicians. Do not neglect your own responsibility for seeking and following sound medical advice, which could go a long way toward relieving your depression. An experienced Christian counselor can wisely guide you through this process.

Symptoms of Depression

8. Elijah's depressive episode gives us a glimpse at a few of the many well-documented symptoms of depression. Which of the following can you personally identity with to some degree? (Check all that apply.) Share your responses with the group.

❏ Low level of energy; lack of motivation; or even exhaustion
❏ Difficulty getting to sleep or inability to sleep through the night
❏ Wanting to sleep constantly; great difficulty getting out of bed
❏ Loss of interest or pleasure in daily activities, sex, and even special occasions
❏ Very little appetite or feeling nauseous; losing weight
❏ Overeating; gaining weight
❏ Feeling irritable; overreacting to small things
❏ Feelings of sadness often accompanied by weeping; feeling empty
❏ Feeling overwhelmed and unable to take action
❏ Difficulty concentrating and completing a task
❏ Feelings of hopelessness or pessimism about the future
❏ Thoughts of death; wishing to die
❏ Fleeting or serious thoughts about hurting oneself
❏ Feelings of worthlessness or inappropriate guilt

9. Which one or two symptoms from this list are particularly prevalent when you're depressed? How do they express themselves in your life?

NOTE: In later sessions we'll explore and choose strategies for coping with these depressive symptoms. We want to avoid any quick-fix schemes, which often result in negative side effects and consequences. We'll also discuss the spiritual dimension of depression later on.

EMBRACING THE TRUTH – 25-30 MINUTES

> LEADER: The goal of "Embracing the Truth" is that group members begin to integrate the truths they're discovering into their personal lives. Be aware that levels of past or current depression will vary among members, so each person's rate and depth of life application could vary greatly from others in the group.

UNHEALTHY METHODS OF COPING

As with any undesirable feeling or experience, we instinctively look for ways to cope with depression. Below are some unhealthy ways that many people seek to cope with the pain of depression:

- ❏ Isolation; social withdrawal from others
- ❏ Avoiding God
- ❏ Overeating comfort food
- ❏ Hours of mindless TV watching
- ❏ Use of alcohol or drugs
- ❏ Buying and spending
- ❏ Multiple or lengthy naps
- ❏ Viewing violent or pornographic material
- ❏ Excessive use of Internet or video games

1. Look back at Elijah's story. What coping mechanisms did he use in response to his depression?

2. To which of these unhealthy coping strategies are you vulnerable when you need to escape or "numb out"?

3. What do you see as some positive ways to cope with depression?

MEASUREMENT OF PROGRESS

Rising out of the depths of depression is not an either-or, black-or-white, all-or-nothing proposition. There are three measurement scales that are helpful in evaluating symptoms of depression.

INTENSITY   **DURATION**   **FREQUENCY**

For example, many depressed people weep. You don't measure progress in dealing with this symptom by asking, "Did you cry this week or not?" Instead, look at this symptom more comprehensively.

1. **INTENSITY:** There's a difference between quiet weeping and body-wracking wailing that wakes the neighbors.
2. **DURATION:** Improvement can mean that instead of crying uncontrollably for one straight hour, you wept for 30 minutes. That's progress!
3. **FREQUENCY:** Is having weeping episodes three times this past week an improvement over crying every day the previous week? You bet it is.

4. Take a few moments and review the list of symptoms for depression on page 12. Choose a symptom you're currently experiencing or have recently experienced. Jot down a few words to describe your current situation with that symptom using the three measurements:

a. Intensity: _____
_____
_____

b. Duration: _____
_____
_____

c. Frequency: _____
_____
_____

NOTE: During the course of this group experience and beyond you're encouraged to use this three-fold measurement device as one of several indicators of your progress.

SETBACKS AND PLATEAUS ON YOUR JOURNEY

Setbacks are normal and even expected. It would certainly be wonderful if the charted line of emotional healing looked like this ...

a steady, smooth line sloping ever upward over time

The reality is that the graph line of emotional improvement looks more like a lightning bolt, a jagged line of progress, plateaus, setbacks, and then more progress.

5. As an example, think about your mood over the past week. What was probably your best day or brightest moment? What was a particularly low point or difficult day? Was there a day this that was neither great nor terrible, just rather average?

Highs and lows, bumps and plateaus are pretty normal. Everyone has them. However, people experiencing depression often misinterpret these normal fluctuations.

6. How do you feel when you experience an emotional setback?
   How does this affect your progress?

It's vital during a setback not to misinterpret the moment and say, "I'm right back where I started from. See, I'm not getting any better!" Setbacks are a predictable part of the healing journey. Think of setbacks as uninvited guests, not permanent residents. Acknowledge the setback, learn from it, and move on.

Plateaus—repetitive days with seemingly no change—don't have to be treated as "places where I'm stuck." Tour de France racing cyclists welcome plateaus as opportunities to rest before climbing the imposing mountains of the Alps.

CONNECTING – 15-20 MINUTES

> LEADER: Use the "Connecting" time to help group members connect with each other, with God, and with their own hearts. Set the tone for openness and trust. Encourage people to begin supporting one another in prayer and in other more tangible ways.

LOST AND FOUND

> LEADER INSTRUCTIONS FOR THE GROUP EXPERIENCE: Give each person a 4" x 6" index card or blank sheet of paper. Explain to group members that they're going to participate in a brief writing exercise and will be invited to share their responses with the group.

Imagine that you're placing a "lost" ad in the Lost and Found section of your newspaper. Describe your depressing personal losses in an imaginary ad. If you're willing, you may then share your ad with the group. Here are a couple ad examples:

"Superpowers have been stolen from Gotham City superhero. Barely able to leap out of bed in a single bound. Energy and enthusiasm have been zapped. Unable to maintain relationships. Productivity at work is suffering. Struggling to hold on; antidote for brain fog needed urgently. E-mail me at superhero@wasted.com.

"Husband lost to infidelity and divorce in the Nashville area. Also missing are peace, joy, and self-esteem. Dreams of our 20th wedding anniversary ran away. Dreams of the future have been replaced by nightmares and insomnia. If ability to hope again is found, please return call Angela at (444) 444-444. A reward is offered."

After a few group members share their personal "lost" ads, discuss the following questions:

1. In writing from this objective perspective, what parts of your story did you see in a different light?

2. What do you feel you have lost either as a cause or result of your depression? What feels as though it's been stolen from you?

3. The writer of the example ad hopes to recover peace, joy, self-esteem, and hope. What do you hope to recover? What are some of the deepest longings you feel?

Let's seek out some powerful help as we ask God to help you to recover or replace some of what feels lost or stolen. How can we pray for you today?

MY PRAYER REQUESTS:

MY GROUP'S PRAYER REQUESTS:

LEADER: *Thank people for coming and encourage them that you're all on this journey together. Let them know that you and the leadership team are available for support. Be sure to give an overview of the "Taking It Home" assignment for the coming week. Strongly encourage everyone to spend time absorbing the truths learned today and completing the assignments for the week, including review of the Group Covenant on page 20 (you'll discuss this next week).*

TAKING IT HOME

At the end of each session of *Beyond the Shadows* are a question for your heart and a question for God. You must have time and solitude for these questions because they are designed to make you listen — to "listen" for the fears and hopes residing in your heart and to "listen" for the urgings of God's Spirit. When you do these exercises, choose a quiet place where you can be alone and thoughtful for at least 20-30 minutes.

LOOKING INWARD: QUESTIONS TO TAKE TO MY HEART

Look into your heart for the answer to these questions. Don't worry about what you ought to feel. Look for the values, hopes, fears, and longings that motivate your most basic thoughts and actions. Every action has a corresponding belief that drives it. Try to be honest about what you believe in the deep recesses of your heart about God, yourself, and the world in which you live.

* How do I feel about accepting the reality that I am experiencing an unexpected, unwanted depression?

* Whether my evaluation is accurate or not, what do I really feel in my heart is the root cause of my depression?

LOOKING UPWARD: A QUESTION TO TAKE TO GOD

Be still and listen for some impression that you sense is from God. Don't manufacture anything. If you sense nothing in the time you allot, so be it. Don't be surprised, however, if something comes to you later as a result of the time you spend "listening."

> ✳ God, when I'm depressed it's hard to think very highly of myself. My confidence and self-worth really takes a hit. What do You like about me? What do You see in me that you wish that I could see?

LOOKING FORWARD: PREPARATION FOR SESSION TWO

Consider these questions to prepare you for the group discussion in Session 2. Capture your thoughts and feelings in the "Misconceptions Journal" on page 21 as you continue on your journey.

1. What is an idea about depression that I've heard or read, and I wonder if it's true?

2. What do I wish that people who've never been depressed understood about depression in general and my depression in particular?

3. What's your response to this statement: "True Christians who are filled with the Holy Spirit, obey God's will, and constantly abide in Christ will not experience depression."?

Group Covenant

As you begin this study, it is important that your group covenant together, agreeing to live out important group values. Once these values are agreed upon, your group will be on its way to experiencing true redemptive community. It's very important that your group discuss these values—preferably as you begin this study.

* PRIORITY: While we are in this group, we will give the group meetings priority. All the sessions are integrated, with each session building on the sessions that precede them. Committed attendance is vital to overcoming your addictions.

  NOTE: Due to the focus of this group on taking the journey to freedom, group sessions will require a full 90 minutes to complete, so plan accordingly.

* PARTICIPATION AND FAIRNESS: Because we are here to receive help, we commit to participation and interaction in the group. No one dominates. We will be fair to others and concentrate on telling our own stories briefly.

* HOMEWORK: The homework experiences are an integral and vital part of the recovery process. The assignments between each session might include: (1) A Question to Take to My Heart; (2) A Question to Take to God; and (3) Activities that must be completed to continue on with your healing journey.

* RESPECT AND OWNERSHIP: Everyone is given the right to his or her own opinions, and all questions are encouraged and respected. We will not judge or condemn as others share their stories. We are each responsible for our own recovery and will not "own" someone else's. Offensive language is not permitted.

* CONFIDENTIALITY: Anything said in our meetings is never repeated outside the meeting without permission of all of group members. This is vital in creating the environment of trust and openness required to facilitate the healing and freedom. Names of attendees will not be shared with others. NOTE: Check state and federal laws governing pastoral and counselor reporting requirements for any known criminal activities.

* LIFE CHANGE: We will regularly assess our progress and will complete the "Taking it Home" activities to reinforce what we are learning and better integrate those lessons into our personal journeys.

* CARE AND SUPPORT: Permission is given to call upon each other at any time, especially in times of crisis. The group will provide care for every member.

* ACCOUNTABILITY AND INTEGRITY: We agree to let the members of our group hold us accountable to commitments we make in whatever loving ways we decide upon. Unsolicited advice giving is not permitted. We will seek out and build a close relationship with accountability partners for mutual growth and responsibility.

* EXPECTATIONS OF FACILITATORS: This meeting is not professional therapy. We are not licensed therapists. Group facilitators are volunteers whose only desire is to encourage people in finding freedom and hope.

I agree to all of the above _____ Date _____

MISCONCEPTIONS JOURNAL

IT

Depression has a weight
to IT, pressing you down
right into the heels of your shoes.

Depression is made of terrible material; IT has
ITs own texture.
IT has a smell that doesn't go away and a sour
taste that lingers at the back of your throat.

Depression has a muffled, muzzled sound
like someone screaming with their mouth duct taped.
IT has a color that is really no color at all because IT has
strangled the light that all colors need in order to breathe.

Depression has a BEGINNING … though I cannot pinpoint
the anniversary. Sometimes it seems as though IT has always been.

Depression has a MIDDLE. I know because I
am in IT.

Depression has an END. It must have an END. Dear God, promise me
that IT has an END. And tell me it's OK to laugh at ITs funeral.

MYTHS AND MISCONCEPTIONS:

DEPRESSION UNVEILED

BREAKING THE ICE – 15-20 MINUTES

LEADER: Encourage each group member to join in the fun. The more connected group members are, the more open and healing the group will become. Keep this time light and fun.
GROUP EXPERIENCE: "Three Truths and a Lie" is a fun way to connect and lead into the topic of deception and misperception. After the icebreakers, invite your group to review and sign the GROUP COVENANT: After the icebreakers, invite your group to review and sign PAGE 20.

1. Enjoy this classic "Three Truths and a Lie" exercise.

   Think of three unusual things about you that no one in the group likely knows (such as childhood experiences, what you wanted to be when you grew up, favorite superhero, a freak accident or injury, an achievement or unique ability, a place you've lived or visited, an unusual job, favorite school subject, or first car or rock concert). Then make up something that stretches the truth but sounds plausible. When it's your turn to tell your "Three Truths and a Lie" in a random order, the rest of the group must guess which statement is false.

2. What made some of the lies seem like truth? What influences can lead us to believe something that isn't true?

There are numerous myths and misconceptions, half-truths and complete falsehoods concerning the causes, the nature, and the treatment of depression. Most untruths are not proclaimed by others with the intent to hurt us. They just don't know the truth so they are merely voicing their opinions or repeating what they've heard. It's our intent in this session to expose the falsehoods and allow the truth to set you free.

Opening Prayer

God, we hear and read so many different things about depression that it's hard to know what to believe. Then there's my own depression and that gets even more confusing. Help us to sort through false information, false declarations, and our own false beliefs. Lead us to truth about depression, about ourselves, and about the way Your see us. On those inevitable days when we're in the pit, we wish we could hide from everyone, including You. We don't really want others to know we're depressed because it's hardly a way to impress anyone. Help us to hear Your gentle, reassuring voice that dispels our shame and removes the need to hide.

Objectives for this Session

- Understand the power of beliefs
- Expose some common falsehoods about depression
- Remove some of the shame and stigma sometimes associated with depression
- Replace falsehoods with truths about depression
- Get us started toward health armed with truth

Discovering the Truth – 35-40 minutes

LEADER: *ASK if anyone would like to share from questions to God and their Hearts. "Discovering the Truth" delves into 10 key myths about depression. Ask volunteers to read Bible passages aloud. You may also want to enlist group members to read some of the myths aloud. Be sure to leave time for Embracing the Truth" and "Connecting." Encourage the group that you're moving along.*

REFILLING OUR TANKS

THE POWER OF BELIEFS

Winston Churchill once remarked, *"A lie can travel halfway around the world before truth can put its pants on."* Half-truths, full-blown lies, myths, and misconceptions about depression abound. These myths, at best, only confuse those struggling with depression. At worst, they have the power to compound depression with harsh judgment that produces feelings of shame, guilt, inadequacy, failure, and unworthiness.

[17] For God did not send his Son into the world to condemn the world, but to save the world through him. ... [20] Everyone who does evil hates the light, and will not come into the light for fear that his deeds will be exposed.

JOHN 3:17,20, NIV

[Jesus clearly explained:] You will know the truth and the truth will set you free.

JOHN 8:32, HCSB

1. Discuss ways that secrets, shame, and shadows can block us from reaching the ongoing life, salvation (John 3:17-20), and freedom (John 8:32) that Jesus wants for each of us.

If truth sets you free, then deeply embedded deception keeps you in bondage. We become enslaved as we live out of deeply held, subtle lies, which in turn drive our choices and behaviors. Because the deceptions are subtle they can sneak up on us and infiltrate our thinking without our awareness. Unfortunately our friends are sometimes the source of the myths and misconceptions. They try to help, but unintentionally hurt us. Good intentions don't turn a falsehood into the truth.

2. Discuss this statement from Henry Blackaby: "What you do in response to God's revelation (invitation) reveals what you believe about God." [1]

3. If we believe that something is true, we'll act on that false belief as if it was true. How can we identify deeply held lies (our true beliefs) that have become so familiar we wear them as we would a comfortable pair of shoes?

MYTHS ON THE NATURE OF DEPRESSION

We'll discuss 10 pervasive myths and misconceptions about depression. Unfortunately you've probably encountered some variation of many of them.
(This list is adapted from *New Light on Depression* by David Biebel and Harold Koenig.[2])

MYTH 1: DEPRESSION IS EASY TO IDENTIFY.

Extreme and prolonged sadness is somewhat obvious. However, depression is actually adept at wearing disguises.

Note that one or more of the following can also indicate depression: fatigue, overall lack of interest in daily activities, irritability, sleep problems, loss of appetite, overeating, anxiousness, or difficulty concentrating.

MYTH 2: YOU CHOOSE TO BE DEPRESSED.

You can do things to make depression better or worse, but it's neither fair nor accurate to say you simply decided one day to start being depressed. A possible additional insinuation can be that you're using your depression to your advantage.

MYTH 3: YOU'RE JUST FEELING SORRY FOR YOURSELF.

This statement is similar to the "you choose to be depressed" misconception. Self-pity is a choice. You don't have to pity yourself. Depression is a whole other ballgame. Only someone who hasn't been depressed would suggest you want to feel that way.

4. Think about your own situation and rate the level of impact on your beliefs for each of the three myths about the nature of depression. Circle the closest response for each.

   1 = *I've never believed it or even thought about it*
   2 = *I've occasionally been influenced or bothered by this thought*
   3 = *I've often found myself thinking something like this*
   4 = *I've believed this statement for a long time*
   5 = *I've been significantly hindered by this belief*

   - Depression is easy to identify: 1.....2.....3.....4.....5
   - You choose whether or not to be depressed: 1.....2.....3.....4.....5
   - If you're depressed, you're just feeling sorry for yourself: 1.....2.....3.....4.....5

[1] *Save me, God, for the water has risen to my neck.* [2] *I have sunk in deep mud, and there is no footing; I have come into deep waters, and a flood sweeps over me. ...* [17] *Don't hide Your face from Your servant, for I am in distress. Answer me quickly!*

PSALM 69:1-2,17, HCSB

5. In Psalm 69, David—called a "man after God's own heart"—admits to his state of depression. How does the truth of his words stand in contrast to Myths 2 and 3?

Myths on Causes of Depression

MYTH 4: YOU'RE DEPRESSED BECAUSE OF UNCONFESSED SIN.

There are instances when guilt feelings contribute to depression. However, this myth claims that depression is either God's direct punishment for unconfessed sins or a toxic side effect of unconfessed sin. Depression doesn't have to have anything to do with sin, and you shouldn't feel ashamed because you experience depression. The Book of Job clearly debunks this myth.

MYTH 5: YOU HAVE WEAK FAITH.

This misconception leaves depressed Christ-followers feeling worthless. You might think, "If I had enough faith, was more spiritually mature, or was spiritually disciplined, then I would not be depressed." Biblical history and church history report a roster full of spiritual leaders who experienced profound depression. Great faith and spiritual discipline don't provide a Teflon® coating against depression.

MYTH 6: DEPRESSION IS JUST ANOTHER WORD FOR GRIEF.

Grief can contribute to depression, but many instances of depression have nothing to do with loss or grief. It's a mistake to try to simplify the causes of depression. There are many factors and contributors that interact to cause it.

MYTH 7: DEPRESSION IS SIMPLY ANGER TURNED INWARD.

This is an old and shortsighted diagnosis that has no research support. The idea is that anger that's repressed rather than expressed backfires on us in the form of depression. As one misguided theorist explained it, "A soldier holding a live hand grenade must throw it lest it explode in his own hand." Hebrews 12:14-15 warns, however, that unresolved anger can turn to bitterness.

6. Again, thinking about your own situation, rate the level of impact on your beliefs for each of the four myths about the causes of depression. Circle the closest response for each myth.

  1 = *I've never believed it or even thought about it*
  2 = *I've occasionally been influenced or bothered by this thought*
  3 = *I've often found myself thinking something like this*
  4 = *I've believed this statement for a long time*
  5 = *I've been significantly hindered by this belief*

- You're depressed because of unconfessed sins.   1.....2.....3......4.....5
- Depressed believers have weak faith.   1.....2.....3......4.....5
- Depression is just another word for grief.   1.....2.....3......4.....5
- Depression is simply anger turned inward.   1.....2.....3......4.....5

[2] Be gracious to me, LORD, for I am weak; heal me, LORD, for my bones are shaking; [3] my whole being is shaken with terror. And You, LORD—how long? [4] Turn, LORD! Rescue me; save me because of Your faithful love. ... [6] I am weary from my groaning; with my tears I dampen my pillow and drench my bed every night. [7] My eyes are swollen from grief; they grow old because of all my enemies.

PSALM 6:2-7, HCSB

7. What are some of the causes of David's depression that he mentions or implies in Psalm 6? Clearly not a man of weak faith, for what is does he cry out to God?

MYTHS ON RECOVERY FROM DEPRESSION

MYTH 8: YOU CAN BEAT DEPRESSION WITH WILLPOWER.

Your will is one key in the treatment of depression, but willpower alone is a weakling fighting a giant. This David doesn't beat this Goliath. Willpower is a one-dimensional tool woefully inadequate to tackle a multi-dimensional condition. You can't even beat something as simple as a cold virus by simply willing it away.

MYTH 9: EVERYONE, ESPECIALLY CHRISTIANS, WILL UNDERSTAND AND SUPPORT YOU.

Though the Bible says to *"weep with those who weep"* and *"comfort one another"* some Christians, especially those who have had no personal experience with depression, may respond in condescending or judgmental ways. Some just don't know what to do or say. They sure don't intend to be distant or unsupportive—they just don't know how help.

MYTH 10: GOD WANTS TO HEAL YOU. IT'S NOT HIS WILL FOR YOU TO BE ON MEDICATION.

This misconception implies that depression results from spiritual problems that are left unresolved when medicine is used. Because the condition is largely invisible and so misunderstood, it's often seen as solely spiritual or emotional. Additionally, in theological circles that pronounce, "It is never God's will for you to be sick," depressed people find ready judgment. Relying on medication is seen as a refusal to trust God. However, these same people would never tell diabetics to throw away their insulin. Medication is one tool, among many, that you may need to tackle depression.

8. Again, thinking about your own situation, rate the level of impact on your beliefs for each of the three myths about treatment of depression. Circle the closest response for each myth.

1 = *I've never believed it or even thought about it*
2 = *I've occasionally been influenced or bothered by that thought*
3 = *I've often found myself thinking something like that*
4 = *I've believed that statement for a long time*
5 = *I've been significantly hindered by that belief*

- You can beat depression with willpower.   1.....2.....3......4......5
- Everyone, especially Christians, will be understanding
  and supportive.   1.....2.....3......4......5
- God wants to heal you. It's not His will for you to be
  dependent upon medication.   1.....2.....3......4......5

KEY POINT: Our God is not simple, we are not simple, life is not simple, and the larger story that we've been born into is not simple.

[13] *I'm standing my ground, GOD, shouting for help, at my prayers every morning, on my knees each daybreak.* [14] *Why, GOD, do you turn a deaf ear? Why do you make yourself scarce?* [15] *For as long as I remember I've been hurting; I've taken the worst you can hand out, and I've had it.* [16] *Your wildfire anger has blazed through my life; I'm bleeding, black and blue.* [17] *You've attacked me fiercely from every side, raining down blows till I'm nearly dead.* [18] *You made lover and neighbor alike dump me; the only friend I have left is Darkness.*

PSALM 88:13-18, THE MESSAGE

9. How does Psalm 88 stand in contrast to the myths about recovery from depression?

[6] *You rejoice in this, though now for a short time you have had to be distressed by various trials* [7] *so that the genuineness of your faith—more valuable than gold, which perishes though refined by fire—may result in praise, glory, and honor at the revelation of Jesus Christ.*

1 PETER 1:6-7, HCSB

[8] *Be sober! Be on the alert! Your adversary the Devil is prowling around like a roaring lion, looking for anyone he can devour.* [9] *Resist him, firm in the faith, knowing that the same sufferings are being experienced by your brothers in the world.* [10] *Now the God of all grace, who called you to His eternal glory in Christ Jesus, will personally restore, establish, strengthen, and support you after you have suffered a little.*

1 PETER 5:8-10, HCSB

10. As you consider Psalm 88 and 1 Peter 1 and 5, what might be some reasons that a loving God would allow suffering and depression in our lives? There's a villain in the story. What role does he play in all this?

Embracing the Truth – 20-25 Minutes

LEADER: *This section focuses on helping group members integrate what they've learned from the Bible and group discussions into their own hearts and lives. The focus continues on our beliefs.*

In having a right approach to depression, consider the words of the Apostle Paul. This is our anchor passage for this entire series of lessons on depression:

7 Now we have this treasure [the glory of God] in clay jars, so that this extraordinary power may be from God and not from us. 8 We are pressured in every way but not crushed; we are perplexed but not in despair; 9 we are persecuted but not abandoned; we are struck down but not destroyed.

2 CORINTHIANS 4:7-9, HCSB

1. What is the point the Bible is making by comparing people to jars of clay? What does the "jars of clay" analogy imply about our susceptibility to depression and our need for help in dealing with it?

Look again at verses 8 and 9 in 2 Corinthians 4. The literary technique Paul employs is a series of four good news/bad news couplets.

2. Discuss how the four sets of reality can apply to our health and difficult conditions like depression.

3. In John 16:33 Jesus promises, *"I've told you all this so that trusting me, you will be unshakable and assured, deeply at peace. In this godless world you will continue to experience difficulties. But take heart! I've conquered the world"* (*The Message*). How does that help you understand how 2 Corinthians 4:8-9 can be true? How does this make you feel?

4. How does Jesus' confident statement that He has overcome or conquered the world help me in a world where I'm guaranteed trouble?

5. Whoa now! In 2 Corinthians 4:8 Paul says, *"We are perplexed but not in despair."* Yet earlier in this same letter (1:8) Paul writes, *"we were completely overwhelmed—beyond our strength—so that we even despaired of life."* If that isn't a contradiction, how do we make sense of it?

6. Clearly Jesus and Paul are not promising me a life with no despair. What then can we expect and on what can we set our hopes?

Jesus Himself admitted to severe agony in the Garden of Gethsemane: *"My soul is overwhelmed with sorrow to the point of death?"* (Matthew 26:38, NIV). Jesus' words should not be spiritualized away; His wrenching soul pain testifies to Christ's humanity but does nothing to diminish His deity. The experiences of Jesus and Paul confirm that feelings of despair are normal. They also encourage us that we don't have to stay stuck in the pit of despair. Cling to that hope in the face of your darkest feelings. That hope is a real light at the end of a tunnel that seems longer than it actually is. Don't give up.

CHRIST-FOLLOWERS HAVE THREE SURE HOPES.

(1) Hebrews quotes Jesus saying, *"I will never leave you or forsake you."* God never abandons us, but is always walking beside us, even in our darkest hours.

(2) We have great reasons not to remain stuck in the pit of despair. In 1 Thessalonians 4:13, Paul explains our hope: *"so you will not grieve like people who have no hope"* (NLT).

(3) God will one day restore the paradise He created us for, removing all our sadness, pain, and sorrow. *"There will be no more death or mourning or crying or pain"* (Rev. 21:4, NIV).

CONNECTING – 15-20 MINUTES

LEADER: *Remind group members "Connecting" is a time to connect with one another, with God, and with their own hearts. The scene you'll show from* The Fugitive *is serious. Be sure to end on a positive and hopeful note. Feel free to use olive oil for anointing purposes in your prayer time.*

THE TRUTH WILL SET YOU FREE!

Remember, if we believe a lie is true, we'll act on that false belief as if it was true. The beliefs we accept exert a powerful influence on the way we live and respond to difficulties.

LEADER INSTRUCTIONS FOR THE GROUP EXPERIENCE: *Have a TV/DVD player set up. Read the following introduction to the group, then play a scene from the film* The Fugitive, *starring Harrison Ford (1993). Show Scene 3, "Trial and Sentencing" (9:40 to 12:58 minutes on the DVD timer). After showing the clip, discuss the following questions.*

In the movie, *The Fugitive*, Richard Kimble (Harrison Ford) is a successful, vascular surgeon who returns home one evening to find his wife dying from a brutal attack and a mysterious one-armed man with a prosthetic arm escaping. Despite his attempts to save her and his testimony about the one-armed man, Kimble faces the charge of first-degree murder, due to evidence such as a misunderstood 9-1-1 call, his fingerprints found "on the lamp, the gun, and the bullets," and no signs of forced entry by the one-armed man.

1. The prosecutor claimed, "ironclad proof" and "indisputable scientific evidence" that Dr. Kimble brutally murdered his wife. What logical conclusion would you draw from the evidence presented in the trial? How convincing was the prosecutor's case?

2. What is Dr. Kimble's emotional state after the death of his beloved wife? In what ways did the lie swirling around him affect him and literally hold him captive?

3. What lies are you beginning to recognize that have held you captive emotionally, mentally, physically, or spiritually? Describe the impact of these lies on your life and choices.

Unlike Dr. Kimble in the movie, we don't have to fight our shadows alone! We should never underestimate the power of a community of faith that understands and supports one another. James 5:14-16 encourages us:

Is anyone among you sick? He should call for the elders of the church, and they should pray over him after anointing him with olive oil in the name of the Lord. The prayer of faith will save the sick person, and the Lord will raise him up; and if he has committed sins, he will be forgiven. Therefore, confess your sins to one another and pray for one another, so that you may be healed. The intense prayer of the righteous is very powerful.

4. Sometimes God responds to our prayers instantly and at other times He chooses a slower or delayed response. While we cannot comprehend the mind of God, we do know that prayer is powerful. In what specific ways can this group pray for you today?

My Prayer and Support Needs:

My Group's Prayer and Support Needs:

Taking It Home

> LEADER: *Remind your group that "Taking it Home" activities are essential to the recovery process. Highlight the importance of keeping a daily journal of thoughts, feelings, and key insights God reveals. Journaling is a powerful tool in the healing journey.*

At the end of each session of *Beyond the Shadows* are a question for your heart and a question for God. You must have time and solitude for these questions because they are designed to make you listen—to "listen" for the fears and hopes residing in your heart and to "listen" for the urgings of God's Spirit. When you do these exercises, choose a quiet place where you can be alone and thoughtful for at least 30 minutes.

LOOKING INWARD: A QUESTION TO TAKE TO MY HEART

Don't worry about what you ought to feel. Look for the values, hopes, fears, and longings that motivate your most basic thoughts and actions. Remember, our behaviors are the best indicator of what we truly believe in our innermost being (Psalm 51:6). Be sure to journal your thoughts, struggles, and insights.

✳ What lies have I believed about myself, God, or my situation? What really is my single greatest fear about going through depression?

LOOKING UPWARD: A QUESTION TO TAKE TO GOD

Now, it's time to ask God a question. Be careful not to rush or manufacture an answer. Don't write down what you think the "right" answer is. Don't turn the Bible into a reference book or spiritual encyclopedia. Just pose a question to God and wait for Him. Anything God speaks will always be consistent with the Scripture. Be sure to write down what you hear from God.

✳ Jesus, You once said that You were "overwhelmed with sorrow to the point of death." How do You want feel about me and the ordeal I'm going through? What do You want me to understand about my emotional pain?

NOTES

1. Henry T. Blackaby and Claude V. King, *Experiencing God Workbook*, (Nashville: LifeWay Press, 1990.)
2. David Biebel & Harold Koenig, *New Light on Depression*, (Grand Rapids: Zondervan, 2004) pp. 75-93.

Looking Forward: Prepare for Session Three

Consider these questions to prepare you for the group discussion in Session 3. Capture your thoughts and feelings in the "Anxiety Journal" as you continue on your journey.

1. Many people experience anxiety along with their depression. How true has this been in my experience?

2. What is currently provoking the greatest worry or anxiety in my life?

3. What have I been told or how do I think I'm supposed deal with anxiety?

4. When Paul says in Philippians 4:6-7: "don't be anxious about anything but pray about everything" (paraphrased), what is my honest response to Paul's admonition?

Anxiety Journal

Wake-up Call

I hide under the covers from a loud sunrise,

too lethargic, too apathetic to move.

I want the whole world to leave me alone.

But my heart is racing, my pulse is running

around inside my body, screaming ...

"Get up! Get up! You've got work to do,

e-mails to send, phone calls to return ...

meetings to dread, appointments to cancel,

smiles to fake, quotas to meet, reports to submit ...

people to avoid, assignments to fumble,

projects to drop, promises to break, ...

bosses to appease, hoops to jump through,

walls to crash into, naps to sneak in ...

coffee to drink, failures to accumulate.

Get up! GET UP! You don't have time to be depressed.

You're carpooling with Anxiety today and you're already late!"

ANXIETY HITCHES A RIDE:

TANDEM ISSUES

BREAKING THE ICE – 15-20 MINUTES

1. Which of the following statements would cause you the greatest worry? Why?

   ❏ Your dentist saying, "I think we're looking at a root canal."
   ❏ Your son saying, "Before you see the car, let me explain."
   ❏ Your in-laws saying, "We'll just be staying for a week ... or so."
   ❏ Your wife saying, "Let's wallpaper the kitchen ourselves."
   ❏ Your husband saying, "You won't believe the deal I got on a new motorcycle!"
   ❏ Your boss saying, "Come on in and close the door."
   ❏ Your mother saying, "He seemed so nice I gave him your phone number."

2. Which of the following best describes your strategy for responding to anxiety?

   ❏ Lie awake at night and imagine the worst
   ❏ Attack it with busyness
   ❏ Gnaw my fingernails to the quick, and then start on my toenails
   ❏ Smother the worry with chocolate or other "guilty pleasures"
   ❏ Distract myself with entertainment
   ❏ Why just worry when you can upgrade to a panic attack
   ❏ Talk it out and get feedback
   ❏ Other: _____

3. From the following topics number the "Top Three" which currently (or typically) provoke the most anxiety in your life.

   ❏ Finances   ❏ Children   ❏ Career   ❏ Ex-spouse
   ❏ Spouse   ❏ Family member   ❏ Parent(s)   ❏ Decisions
   ❏ Health   ❏ Neighbors   ❏ Relational issues at work or church
   ❏ Other: _____

Often it feels like anxiety is riding a tandem bicycle with depression. Either depression or anxiety alone would make it hard enough to cope with, but a hybrid of the two can be brutal. Whether you're currently experiencing some of the stronger symptoms of anxiety or you just find yourself occasionally ambushed by worry, this session will be helpful.

OPENING PRAYER

Lord, we don't have to try to worry. Panic seems to come to us naturally. Depression is bad enough and then anxiety attacks us. It's like some two-headed monster and our sword seems so small. We are too frail to fight this battle alone. Jesus, Prince of Peace, meet us in our group. Calm the raging storm inside our souls and give us Your peace that mysteriously overcomes the world

OBJECTIVES FOR THIS SESSION

- Rightly understand scriptural teaching ans human research about anxiety
- Understand the relationship between our needs, fears, and anxieties
- Learn to expose and confront our anxieties
- Recognize the amazing role of authentic prayer in overcoming anxiety

DISCOVERING THE TRUTH – 35-40 MINUTES

LEADER: ASK what group members realized this week about fears and lies they've believed. "Discovering the Truth" revolves around the often-quoted verse about anxiety: Philippians 4:6. Read the introductory paragraphs and questions aloud. Invite volunteers to read the Bible verses. Leave ample time for "Embracing the Truth" questions and the "Connecting" group experience. Briefly review the "Refilling Our Tanks" process.

REFILLING OUR TANKS

You've Gotta Be Kidding! Right?

One of the best-selling books of 1998 was *Don't Sweat the Small Stuff*. Author Richard Carlson tapped into feelings of panic over the consuming stress of everyday modern life. Our technological society has discovered that the evil twin of rapid development is rampant anxiety. Therapists not only treat hundreds of thousands of adults with anxiety disorders, but they now face anxiety in young children, most from financially secure homes, who demonstrate symptoms not even seen in children from war-torn nations!

Into our chaos we hear the Apostle Paul say, "Do not be anxious about anything" (Philippians 4:6, NIV), and something inside us wants to scream, "Oh yeah? Get real, buddy!" *Don't Sweat the Small Stuff* claims, "It's all small stuff." But when your 80 year-old mother who lives 300 miles away falls and breaks her hip, it's not small stuff. When your spouse is laid off, it's not small stuff. When your oldest daughter separates from her husband, it's not small stuff. When your child steals jewelry from a store, it's not small stuff. And when it all happens in the same week, it's definitely not small stuff!

1. Recall a time when a difficult or shocking event caused sudden anxiety that gave way to a lasting depressed state. Share your feelings and coping strategies with the group.

6 Do not be anxious about anything, but in everything, by prayer and petition, with thanksgiving, present your requests to God. 7 And the peace of God, which transcends all understanding, will guard your hearts and your minds in Christ Jesus.

PHILIPPIANS 4:6-7, NIV

2. Is Paul really instructing us never to worry? Is he condemning worry for true followers of Christ?

Paul was in jail facing the possibility of execution when he wrote the Philippian letter. That makes his recommendation in verses 6-7 credible. Paul knows personally that life is tough and worries will come. Rather than condemning anxiety, what he gives is us a prescription for dealing with our worries.

Two Types of Anxiety

Social scientists and counselors make a useful distinction between two types of anxiety.

1. **Stress Anxiety**: This a function of "high adrenaline, caused by over-extension and stress, which depletes the brain's natural tranquilizers and sets the stage for high anxiety."[1]

2. **Worry Anxiety**: This involves an "overestimation of the probability of danger and exaggeration of its degree of terribleness."[2] Worry-induced anxiety—*merimnao* in the Greek—is the focus of Paul's encouragement in Philippians 4:6-7. Consider other verses that use *merimnao* …

*Do not be **anxious** (merimnao) about anything …*

PHILIPPIANS 4:6, NIV

*[19] But I hope in the Lord Jesus to send Timothy to you shortly, so that I also may be encouraged when I learn of your condition. [20] For I have no one else of kindred spirit who will genuinely be **concerned** (merimnao) for your welfare.*

PHILIPPIANS 2:19-20, NASB

*Then, besides all this, I have the daily burden of my **concern** (merimnao) for all the churches.*

2 CORINTHIANS 11:28, NLT

3. How wide a range of meanings—positive and negative—do you see in Paul's usage of the verb *merimnao*? What do you suppose is the difference between the *merimnao* we're not supposed to have and the *merimnao* that Paul commends in Timothy?

4. In Philippians 4:6-7, Paul advises that prayer is the effective antidote to worry anxiety. What do you think needs to be true of our communication with God for it to act as a soother of our troubled hearts and minds?

[Jesus' instruction about anxiety:] ²⁵ *That is why I tell you not to worry about everyday life—* *whether you have enough food and drink, or enough clothes to wear. Isn't life more than food, and* *your body more than clothing?* ²⁶ *Look at the birds. They don't plant or harvest or store food in barns,* *for your heavenly Father feeds them. And aren't you far more valuable to him than they are?* ²⁷ *Can* *all your worries add a single moment to your life? ...* ³³ *Seek the Kingdom of God above all else, and* *live righteously, and he will give you everything you need.* ³⁴ *So don't worry about tomorrow, for* *tomorrow will bring its own worries. Today's trouble is enough for today.*

MATTHEW 6:25-27,33-34, NLT

5. How does Jesus' instruction for dealing with worry anxiety build on Paul's advice? What do we need to believe about ourselves and about God to successfully pull this off?

STRESS-INDUCED ANXIETY

Worry-induced anxiety is an emotional response to concerns about the future. However, there's a deadlier anxiety that is a more physical response to stress in the present. Stress-induced anxiety is related to fear. This high anxiety leaves you feeling overwhelmed and unable to cope with either the *type* or the sheer *number* of tasks at hand.

NEEDS, FEARS, AND ANXIETIES

We have two primary emotional needs: the need for *significance* and the need for *security*. We want to feel our lives are worthwhile, and we want to feel safe. Our most basic fears cluster around these needs.

The Need for Significance Encompasses:

- Fear of disapproval, criticism, or being ignored
- Fear of not measuring up or not meeting expectations;
- Fear of failure
- Fear of being controlled by others

The Need for Security Encompasses:

- Fear of rejection or abandonment
- Fear of poverty
- Fear of injury or death

6. What kinds of situations have you found to produce the greatest levels of stress anxiety for you? How would you relate these stressors to the chart of needs and fears?

5 If you need wisdom, ask our generous God, and he will give it to you. He will not rebuke you for asking. 6 But when you ask him, be sure that your faith is in God alone. Do not waver, for a person with divided loyalty is as unsettled as a wave of the sea that is blown and tossed by the wind. 7 Such people should not expect to receive anything from the Lord. 8 Their loyalty is divided between God and the world, and they are unstable in everything they do.

JAMES 1:5-8, NLT

7. James, too, points to going to God as the solution for anxiety. How can we pray with "divided loyalty" or with our faith *not* "in God alone"? Why is this totally ineffective?

8. In our search for His peace that can guard our hearts and minds, what insights can we gain from the Needs–Fears Chart and James' warning about talking to God?

EMBRACING THE TRUTH – 20-25 MINUTES

THE HEART OF STRESS ANXIETY

> LEADER: *This section focuses on helping group members integrate what they've learned from the Bible discussions into their own hearts and lives. The group will focus on exposing and confronting anxiety. A key to overcoming anxiety is replacing lies we've believed with truth.*

Much of what causes us **worry anxiety** is launched from conversations we have with others. However, it's the silent, internal conversations that most often script our **stress anxiety**.

Pastor and psychologist William Backus defines anxiety as:

- Fear in the absence of real danger,
- Over-estimation of the probability and degree of danger, and
- Imagined negative results.[3]

1. What do you think of Backus' definition of anxiety? With which part of it do you identify most strongly?

2. Tell of a time when you were so concerned about how something might turn out that you had serious trouble making yourself face it.

We aren't saying truly terrible things never happen. We are saying that we often exaggerate how badly things might turn out and underestimate our ability to cope.

RENOUNCING FALSE BELIEFS

Our anxieties can be compared to a plate of spaghetti—all tangled up. Some worries are on the surface; others are buried deep in the pile. Somewhere in it all is the meatball— the root worry about some perceived threat to our significance or security. It helps to distinguish surface and root worries and acknowledge them to God. *"Unbelief talks to itself instead of talking to God,"* writes Brooklyn Tabernacle pastor Jim Cymbala.[4] God gives us some key truths we must embed deeply in our hearts if we want to connect effectively with God.

[1] Don't be afraid, I've redeemed you. I've called your name. You're mine. [2] When you're in over your head, I'll be there with you. When you're in rough waters, you will not go down. When you're between a rock and a hard place, it won't be a dead end— [3] because I am GOD, your personal God, the Holy of Israel, your Savior. I paid a huge price for you: all of Egypt, with rich Cush and Seba thrown in! [4] That's how much you mean to me! That's how much I love you! I'd sell off the whole world to get you back, trade the creation just for you.

ISAIAH 43:1B-4, THE MESSAGE

3. According to Isaiah 43, what truths about yourself does God want you to fully embrace as you approach Him in dealing with your fears and anxieties? How can this keep you from divided loyalty and double-mindedness that James 1 highlights?

13 That's right. Because I, your GOD, have a firm grip on you and I'm not letting go. I'm telling you, "Don't panic. I'm right here to help you." 14 Do you feel like a lowly worm, Jacob? Don't be afraid. Feel like a fragile insect, Israel? I'll help you. I, GOD, want to reassure you. The God who buys you back, The Holy of Israel.

ISAIAH 41:13-14, THE MESSAGE

28 Do you not know? Have you not heard? The Everlasting God, the LORD, the Creator of the ends of the earth does not become weary or tired. His understanding is inscrutable. 29 He gives strength to the weary, and to him who lacks might He increases power. 30 Though youths grow weary and tired, and vigorous young men stumble badly, 31 yet those who wait for the LORD will gain new strength; they will mount up with wings like eagles, they will run and not get tired, they will walk and not become weary.

ISAIAH 40:28-31, NASB

4. **God also wants us to fully embrace the truth about Him.** What key truths about God jump out from Isaiah 40:28-31 and 41:13-14? How would your prayers and emotions change if you fully embraced these truths?

5. According to Isaiah 40:29-31, does God always keep stress out of our lives or move to eliminate it as soon as we cry out to Him? What do you see as the key to having hope and confidence when stress or panic hits?

CONNECTING – 20-25 MINUTES

CONFRONTING OUR ANXIETIES

Take 10-15 minutes **on your own** to respond to the following questions, and then in question 4 write a brief prayer to God.

1. What would you say are some of your surface worries that are frequently in the front of your mind?

2. Ask God to help you see some of the hidden worries that usually lurk below the level of your consciousness? At this stage of your journey, what do you think might be the root worry that sets the stage for the rest of your worries?

3. Refer back to the Needs–Fears Chart on page 40. Connect some of your surface or hidden fears to the core need for Significance or the need for Security. Then make the connection to your corresponding primary fears in that chart.

4. Write a prayer to God expressing your deepest fears, confident in your personal value to Him and acknowledging your hope in His power and desire for your best ... no matter how circumstances seem.

LEADER: *Gently pull the group back together to discuss the final questions. Make yourself available for those who need to talk or pray after the session.*

---

5. Which of the primary fears are you finding has the strongest grip on your heart?

Look once more at Philippians 4:6-7. *Do not be anxious about anything, but in everything, by prayer and petition, with thanksgiving, present your requests to God. And the peace of God, which transcends all understanding, will guard your hearts and your minds in Christ Jesus.* Notice that God's peace that "transcends all understanding" is the **prayer result**, not the **prayer request** we take to God.

6. If you're comfortable, read the prayer you've started writing to God. How can this group support you in prayer and practical support this week?

My Prayer and Support Needs:

My Group's Prayer and Support Needs:

TAKING IT HOME

Worry negatively anticipates the future. Guilt negatively reviews the past. Both are worthless unless they motivate us to do something differently in the present. As the saying goes, "Worrying does not empty tomorrow of its troubles; it only empties today of its strength." In Jesus' words: "Can all your worries add a single moment to your life?" (Matthew 6:25). This week let your worry drive you to your knees in prayer.

LOOKING INWARD: A QUESTION TO TAKE TO MY HEART

Look into your heart for the answers to these questions. Don't worry about what you *ought* to feel. Look for the values, hopes, fears, and longings that motivate your most basic thoughts and actions. Every action has a corresponding belief that drives it. Try to draw out what you believe in the deep recesses of your heart about God, yourself, and the world in which you live.

> ✳ Beneath the layers of more surface and perhaps obvious worries, what fears lurk and haunt me from deep inside? What past hurts or events are driving my feelings?

LOOKING UPWARD: A QUESTION TO TAKE TO GOD

Be still and listen to God; He consistently encourages us to wait with expectation. Be careful not to rush or manufacture an answer. Don't write down what you think the "right" answer is. Don't turn the Bible into a reference book or spiritual encyclopedia. Just pose a question to God and wait for Him. Anything God speaks will always be consistent with the Scripture. Be sure to write down what you hear from God.

✳ Almighty God, I'm so thankful that You have a solid grip on me. What do You want to say to me about my core fears and deep anxiety? What beliefs do You want to put right?

LOOKING FORWARD: PREPARATION FOR SESSION FOUR

Consider these questions to prepare you for the group discussion in Session 4. Capture your thoughts and feelings in the "Stinking Thinking & Right Thinking Journal" on page 49 as you continue on your journey.

1. Which of these best describes my thinking when I'm depressed?
   a. Pessimistic
   b. Hopeless
   c. Optimistic
   d. Gloomy
   e. Somewhat negative
   f. Critical
   g. Still hopeful
   h. Other: _____

2. About which of the following am I prone to getting down on myself?
   a. My competence
   b. My personality
   c. My finances
   d. My self-discipline
   e. My intelligence
   f. My appearance
   g. My value to others
   h. My career

3. The Bible says, "Be transformed by the renewing of your mind" (Romans 12:2). How can I apply this in my daily life?

4. What is something I've changed my mind about because of my faith in God? How did the change come about?

NOTES

1. Archibald Hart, *The Anxiety Cure* (Nashville: Word Publishing, 1999), p. 6.
2. William Backus and Marie Chapian, *Telling Yourself the Truth* (Minneapolis: Bethany House, 1980), p. 68.
3. William Backus and Marie Chapian, *Telling Yourself the Truth* (Minneapolis: Bethany House, 1980).
4. Jim Cymbala, *Fresh Faith* (Grand Rapids, MI: Zondervan, 1999), p. 93.

STINKING THINKING & RIGHT THINKING JOURNAL

In the middle of the journey of our life
I found myself in a dark wood for I had lost the right path.

— Dante

How did I get here? I don't mean an explanation with
empty words like biochemical, norepinephrine,
serotonin, dopamine, neurotransmitters, and cortisol;
Or loaded phrases like psychic disturbance,
chemical imbalance, brain imagining, systemic stress.
I mean how did I get here?

How did I escort myself to this emotional ghetto?
What wrong turn, wrong exit did I take and how far back?

The shopping mall map points to this spot with an arrow
declaring "You are here." I know that! I know where I am!
Tell me how I got here! Please, God, show me how to get out;
And I beg you—don't tell me to go back the way I came.
I cannot bear to walk alone backwards through hell.

Take my hand, grab it
like the hand of a man slipping over the cliff edge.
Hold my hand; swallow it up in Yours.
Tug on my hand; pull hard, sprain my wrist if You must,
but lead me out of this desert maze, lest I wander
like Israel in dry, maddening circles.

CORRECT STINKING THINKING:

TELLING YOURSELF THE TRUTH

BREAKING THE ICE – 10-15 MINUTES

LEADER: Your group should be beginning to gel as people become more comfortable with one another. The "Breaking the Ice" questions give you a lighthearted way to lead into an important discussion about the belief structure that underlies depression. Keep this fun for everyone. Choose only two of the questions to save time.

1. What toy or game from your childhood do you wish you had now in good-as-new condition? Why do you wish you had that one?

2. Which of these old technologies would you find it hardest to adjust to?

   ❑ Wood-burning stove
   ❑ Outhouse
   ❑ Horse and buggy
   ❑ Washboard for washing clothes in the creek
   ❑ Black and white television with antenna on the roof
   ❑ Ink and quill for writing notes that have to be delivered by postal "snail mail"
   ❑ Shared party-line telephone
   ❑ Other: _____

3. If you had the skill to take something old and beat up and restore it to mint condition, what would you enjoy restoring? Why?

   ❑ Furniture   ❑ Cars or trucks   ❑ Boats or airplanes
   ❑ Houses   ❑ Photos or artwork   ❑ Clothing and fashion accessories
   ❑ Vintage typewriter, sewing machine, or phonograph
   ❑ Other: _____

Most of us look back fondly to music and television programs from when we were young. Maybe the heroes of long ago seem braver than today. At the very least, gasoline prices are worth remembering! We call those warm looks back **nostalgia**. The Scriptures seem to hold simultaneously a respect and reverence for the past as well as an emphasis on pressing forward into what's new.

OPENING PRAYER

Dear God, I have ways of thinking that are familiar and automatic. Push Ctrl-P or Command-P and the file goes to the default printer. My mind is like a default printer—it doesn't challenge the data; it just prints it out. And then I react ... with frustration, resentment, discouragement, despair, even hopelessness. I seldom question whether my thinking is accurate. I think. I feel. I react. If I'm going to challenge my thinking and uproot self-defeating false beliefs, I'm going to need Your help. Holy Spirit, please shine Your light on the false beliefs that hide in the dark of my weary mind. Renew my mind with Your truth.

OBJECTIVES FOR THIS SESSION

- Understand the power of stinking thinking
- Comprehend the relationship between beliefs, emotions, and behavior
- Understand the two-step process of mind renewal
- Learn to spot the four categories of self-defeating false beliefs
- Learn to replace lies we believe with truth

DISCOVERING THE TRUTH – 40-45 MINUTES

God declares through His prophet, "See, the former things have taken place, and new things I declare; before they spring into being I announce them to you (Isaiah 42:9, NIV). Sprinkled throughout the Old Testament are exhortations to sing a "new song."

LEADER: ASK about any insights related to anxiety from homework. "Discovering the Truth" will focus first on the old ruts of thinking into which we slide back, and then on the two-step process of mind renewal. Read the text aloud or ask for volunteers. Keep things moving so you leave time for "Embracing the Truth" and "Connecting." Using the "Refilling Our Tanks" gauge, indicate that you're engaging the first of four recovery dimensions

The ABC's of Depression

Realistic thinking is crucial to healthy living because thinking sets the stage for emotions and behavior. Psychological research confirms this sequence: Thoughts, beliefs, and interpretations (**A**) provoke emotions or feelings (**B**), which propel reactions and behavior (**C**). There is a villain in the story who knows how we operate. According to 1 Peter 5:8, "your adversary the Devil" wants more than anything to take you out, and he attacks most fiercely in the area of our thoughts and beliefs.

The ABC sequence, which happens subtly and rapidly, looks like this:

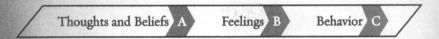

1. Why is it more fundamental to renew our minds than our emotions or behavior? What or whom has had a role in shaping your core thoughts and beliefs? (Think about both the physical and spiritual realms.)

2. What resources does God give us for renewing our minds? How has He done this for you in the past?

FALLING INTO OLD RUTS

We must examine our old ways of thinking, beliefs, attitudes, and reactions that are more worn and beat-up than that old car you got when you were a teen. We tend to fall back into past negative thought processes—what Alcoholics Anonymous calls "stinkin' thinkin'." We need to discover some of the stinkin' thinkin' that feeds depression. This may be subtle, almost instinctual thought patterns that we've relied on for years—maybe decades—and are most likely contributing in big ways to our depression.

[1] As we have received mercy, we do not give up. [2] Instead, we have renounced the shameful, secret things, not walking in deceit or distorting God's message, but in God's sight we commend ourselves to every person's conscience by an open display of the truth. ... [6] For God who said, "Light shall shine out of darkness"—He has shone in our hearts to give the light of the knowledge of God's glory in the face of Jesus Christ.

2 CORINTHIANS 4:1-2,6, HCSB

[1] I urge you, brothers, in view of God's mercy, to offer your bodies as living sacrifices, holy and pleasing to God—this is your spiritual act of worship. [2] Do not conform any longer to the pattern of this world, but be transformed by the renewing of your mind. Then you will be able to test and approve what God's will is—His good, pleasing, and perfect will.

ROMANS 12:1-2, NIV

3. According to 2 Corinthians 4:2, what four things do we need to renounce and ask God to transform (change in our understanding)? What's the prescribed antidote in verses 2 and 6?

4. In Romans 12:1, "brothers" refers to Christ-followers. What two decisions do we need to make in order to allow God to renew our minds and transform us (verses 1 and 2)?

5. J. B. Phillips famously paraphrased Romans 12:2 as follows: *"Don't let the world around you squeeze you into its own mould, but let God re-mould your minds from within."* How can prevalent worldviews brainwash us into thinking contrary to the ways and truth of God?

The word translated "be transformed" comes from the Greek *metanoia*, which means to change (*meta*) our mind-set or understanding (*noia*). The word "metamorphosis" is a related term, meaning a change in form or substance; it's used to describe what occurs when a caterpillar emerges from its cocoon as a butterfly. Given the spectacular change that takes place inside the cocoon, it clear that the transformation takes place from the inside out.

6. Why do you suppose trying to change only externals such as our appearance or surroundings seldom leads to meaningful changes in handling life's struggles?

TWO-STEP RENEWAL

Renewal is always a two-step process: take off the old; replace it with the new. Think about refinishing furniture, restoring a vintage automobile, or reupholstering a couch.

7. Why is removing old finishes or rust so important to restoring an antique piece of furniture or an antique automobile? What will happen if you try to apply a new finish over the old surface?

[17] Live no longer as the Gentiles do, for they are hopelessly confused. [18] Their minds are full of darkness; they wander far from the life God gives because they have closed their minds and hardened their hearts against him. ... [20] But that isn't what you learned about Christ. [21] Since you have heard about Jesus and have learned the truth that comes from him, [22] throw off your old sinful nature and your former way of life, which is corrupted by lust and deception. [23] Instead, let the Spirit renew your thoughts and attitudes. [24] Put on your new nature, created to be like God—truly righteous and holy.

EPHESIANS 4:17-24, NLT

8. Amazingly, God makes us entirely New Creations when we place our faith in Jesus (see also 2 Corinthians 5:17). The only problem is that most of us never experience much of this "new creation." According to Ephesians 4:17-24, why? To which response can you most relate?

   ❏ The enemy, also called the Prince of Darkness has confused us, telling us God doesn't care and we're nothing.
   ❏ We continue to live out of the well-worn patterns and ruts in our lives and don't embrace our new hearts and new lives.
   ❏ We block the work of the Holy Spirit by resisting Him or turning away from God and seeking satisfaction in other lusts and addictions.

9. Describe in your own words the two-step renewal process for our minds and hearts outlined in Ephesians 4:21-24? Brainstorm practical ways you can apply each step.

Our false beliefs, distorted desires, and well-worn paths of behavior create ruts that make life unmanageable. Even after we've surrendered our lives to Jesus, we still carry baggage from our past. We can continue to bury our stories and hurts deep inside, denying their importance, or we can unpack our baggage with God and others we trust.

EMBRACING THE TRUTH – 20-25 MINUTES

> LEADER: *This section focuses on helping group members integrate what they've learned about renewing their minds into their own lives. Be sure that group members take time to share practical ideas that have been helpful.*

Remember Jesus' words in John 8: 32: "*You shall know the truth and the truth will set you free.*" Thinking accurately about life and its problems is an important step toward handling depression. As we reconize the enemy's chief tactic of distrotion, we can fight back.

Dr. William Backus, a Christian psychologist, suggests in *Telling Yourself* the Truth that there are three key areas of false beliefs that can perpetuate depression. We need to be sure to address each of these areas of belief. [1]

FAULTY AND SELF-DEFEATING BELIEFS ABOUT OURSELVES

When we think self-defeating thoughts, we beat ourselves up with self-condemning attacks in one or more of the following areas where we feel vulnerable:

- Competence
- Personality
- Finances
- Self-discipline
- Abilities
- Intelligence
- Appearance
- Value to others or God
- Career
- Character

1. Why do you suppose depressed people are susceptible to self-condemning thinking?

2. In which of the areas listed above are you vulnerable to condemning self-talk? What are some of the condemning thoughts you repeat regularly?

FAULTY AND SELF-DEFEATING BELIEFS ABOUT OUR SITUATIONS

Depressed people also tend to defeat themselves by keeping up inner dialogs in which they paint bleak pictures of their circumstances. Without realizing it, they exaggerate to themselves how bad things are and how much worse they're bound to get.

3. When depressed what are some hypercritical things you've found yourself saying or thinking about your circumstances?

4. Where do you think you learned this way of looking at life? Have you always been a pessimist or have you developed this "skill"?

FAULTY AND SELF-DEFEATING THOUGHTS ABOUT OUR FUTURE

The third area of self-defeating thinking concerns the future. Depressed people tend to see failure and disaster awaiting them. The end result of such fatalistic brooding can be a state of dark hopelessness.

5. How can you imagine negative thinking about the future interfering with recovery from depression?

6. What's the difference between learning from past mistakes and defining the future in terms of past mistakes? Share an example of each.

You're not serving a life-sentence of endless misery. You may actually be in the middle of a season of terrible but temporary pain. However, if you listen to the lies of the enemy, you might begin to agree with some dark beliefs that can keep you in a downward emotional spiral. Most suicidal people reach that point of desperation not because of how bad the present is, but because of how bad they expect the future to become. They start to belive the lies of the "Father of liars" (John 8:44) so they lose heart and hope.

7. What hope for a better future do the following words from God offer? How do you see them applying to you?

¹⁴ All those led by God's Spirit are God's sons. ¹⁵ For you did not receive a spirit of slavery to fall back into fear, but you received the Spirit of adoption, by whom we cry out, "Abba, Father!" ¹⁶ The Spirit Himself testifies together with our spirit that we are God's children, ¹⁷ and if children, also heirs—heirs of God and co-heirs with Christ —seeing that we suffer with Him so that we may also be glorified with Him.

ROMANS 8:14-17, HCSB

"For I know the plans I have for you," says the LORD. "They are plans for good and not for disaster, to give you a future and a hope."

JEREMIAH 29:11, NLT

²² Because of the LORD's great love we are not consumed, for his compassions never fail. ²³ They are new every morning; great is your faithfulness. ²⁴ I say to myself, "the LORD is my portion; therefore I will wait for him." ²⁵ The LORD is good to those whose hope is in him, to the one who seeks him.

LAMENTATIONS 3:22-25, NIV

¹² I know how to live on almost nothing or with everything. I have learned the secret of living in every situation, whether it is with a full stomach or empty, with plenty or little. ¹³ For I can do everything through Christ, who gives me strength.

PHILIPPIANS 4:12-13, NLT

NOTE: We'll focus on God's role and our perspectives of God in our depression in the next session.

CONNECTING – 20-25 MINUTES

> *LEADER INSTRUCTIONS FOR THE GROUP EXPERIENCE: Have a TV/DVD player set up. Read the following introduction to the group, and then play the first half of Scene 11 "A Close Friend" from the 2006 film* Miss Potter, *starring Renee Zellweger and Emily Watson. (1:10:05 to 1:14:24 minutes on the DVD timer — up until Miss Potter signs the deed for the country farm). After showing the clip, discuss the following questions.*

Miss Potter is the charming account of the creator and illustrator of the Peter Rabbit story and many other Victorian children's classics. Thirty-year-old Beatrix had been secretly engaged to her publisher Norman Warne, but tragically he died while she was away in the English lake country with her parents. This scene shows her emotional collapse following Norman's death. Norman's sister Millie knew of the engagement and intervened to rescue Beatrix from black despair.

1. Beatrix couldn't admit or share her grief with anyone but Millie. How did this intensify the abandonment she felt?

2. What was happening in Beatrix' mind that wouldn't let her escape into her work and the fantasy world where all her familiar animal friends lived?

3. Why did Millie want to clean Beatrix up and get her out of that room in which she was staying? What did Millie mean when she said, "I loved him too. But he's gone"?

4. Our tendency when depressed is to withdraw into our own little worlds and spiral deeper; giving more foothold to the enemy. Who helps you get perspective on life when your emotions try to drag you toward depression? How can a group like this one help?

MY PRAYER AND SUPPORT NEEDS:

MY GROUP'S PRAYER AND SUPPORT NEEDS:

TAKING IT HOME

LOOKING INWARD: QUESTIONS TO TAKE TO MY HEART

Here are several common "cognitive distortions" for you to think about this week. "Cognitive distortion" is a ten-dollar technical term for stinking thinking about life. This list is adapted from *Feeling Good: The New Mood Therapy*, by David N. Burns.[2] Consider whether any of these are interfering with your ability to understand your life fairly and accurately. Almost everyone can relate in some way to all 10 cognitive distortions. Try to identify those to which you are especially susceptible.

COGNITIVE DISTORTIONS

All-or-Nothing Thinking: I look at things in black-and-white categories. There are only victories and defeats. The glass is either completely full or it's empty.

Overgeneralization: I view a negative event as a never-ending pattern of defeat. I tend to say things are always this way or never that way.

Mental Filter: I dwell on the negatives and ignore the positives.

Discounting the Positives: I insist that my accomplishments or positive qualities don't count. This may seem similar to Mental Filter. Mental Filter is stuck on the negative, while this distortion ignores the positives.

Jumping to Conclusions: (A) Mind Reading: I assume people are reacting negatively to me when in fact I have no definitive evidence for this. (B) Fortune Telling: I instinctively predict that things will turn out badly. My "crystal ball" seems only to project negative outcomes.

Magnification or Minimization: I blow things way out of proportion, or I shrink their importance. This is also called the "binocular trick." Looking the through the standard end of the emotional binoculars I magnify the Negatives. Viewing the Positives through the opposite end of the binoculars shrinks them to insignificance.

Emotional Reasoning: I give too much authority to my feelings as a reliable interpreter of reality. This can be summarized as "I feel it; therefore, it is true."
"Should" Statements: I mercilessly criticize myself with "I should ..." or "I should have ..." or "I never should have ..."

Labeling: I identify myself by my shortcomings. Instead of saying, "I made a mistake," I tell myself, "I'm a fool," "I'm an idiot," or "I'm a failure."

Personalization or Blame: I completely blame myself for something I wasn't entirely responsible for, or I blame someone else and overlook ways I contributed to the problem.

✳ **Which two or three distortions tend to characterize my thinking? Why?**

✳ How has each of these impacted my ability to handle the pressures of life successfully?

LOOKING UPWARD: A QUESTION TO TAKE TO GOD

Again, be still and listen to God; He wants you to embrace the truth. Just pose a question to God and wait for Him. Anything God speaks will always be consistent with the Scripture. Write down what you hear from God.

✳ God, what memory that I repeatedly rehearse do You wish I would release to You? With what belief or truth would You like me to replace it?

LOOKING FORWARD: PREPARATION FOR SESSION FIVE

In Session Five we'll discuss some of the spiritual dynamics of depression that can leave us feeling at odds with God. It's pretty hard to sense His love and concern when everything around us seems to be falling apart. Consider these questions to prepare you for the group discussion in Session 5. Capture your thoughts and feelings in the "Feelings About God Journal" on page 63.

1. What are my honest feelings about God and my life right now?

2. What are some of the negative thoughts or doubts I've had about God's interest in me during times of depression?

3. How can having negative thoughts about God make me feel less worthy of His love and care? How do I feel about myself right now?

NOTES
1. William Backus and Marie Chapian, *Telling Yourself the Truth*, (Minneapolis: Bethany House, 1982).
2. David D. Burns, Feeling Good: *The New Mood Therapy*, (New York: William Morrow & Company, 1980).

Feelings About God Journal

Extra Junk

I have these two plastic sticks that serve as fences in the grocery line. They clearly define what I've chosen and what I will pay for. I did not choose canned artichoke hearts— they're yours. For the person in front of me, my fence is a boundary of ownership and choice, a way of saying, "Relax, lady, I know that's your Haagen-Dazs®." For the guy behind me, I put my fence down as a way of saying, "Don't crowd my stuff," and in case anyone is looking, that six-pack of Budweiser® is not mine.

(I have corralled my choices.)

But when I reach the cashier, I find there are items in my collection I did not search out. Difficult and painful memories I did not select. Stressors I did not want, and do not want now. I had no "Buy 1 – Get 1 Free" coupon for these inadequacies and failures.

I don't want any of this junk. I did not pluck it from the shelf and put it in my cart.
However, it's mine now. It's not the life of the lady in front of me;
it's not the life of the guy behind me. It's MINE!

God, help me with the cost of this stuff I did not choose.

Help me carry these bulging plastic bags of stuff—

these burdens I did not want.

ENGAGE THE SPIRITUAL:
WRESTLING WITH GOD

In Session Four we considered how we think about our selves, our circumstances, and our futures. We discussed the need to recognize and replace self-defeating patterns of thought with true beliefs and thought patterns. In this session, we'll focus on thoughts, beliefs, and relationships connected with God. We sometimes forget that our physical, mental, and spiritual selves are fully interconnected and deeply affect one another. Depressed people often doubt their lives have meaning. They often doubt the existence of God or conclude that He can't or won't do anything about their emotional struggles.

BREAKING THE ICE – 15-20 MINUTES

LEADER INSTRUCTIONS FOR THE GROUP EXPERIENCE: Have a TV/DVD player set up. Read the "Mighty Complaint" introduction to the group, and then play Scene 5 "Fired" from the 2003 film Bruce Almighty *(the scene runs from 17:20 to 23:02 minutes on the DVD timer). After showing the clip, discuss the following questions.*

MIGHTY COMPLAINT

In the movie *Bruce Almighty*, Bruce Nolan (Jim Carey) is a TV reporter in Buffalo, NY who wants a vacant news anchor position. When the less talented Evan Baxter lands the job and Bruce ends up getting fired, he gets angry and blames God. Bruce looks at what's going wrong in his life and unloads on his girlfriend and God for the unfairness of it all.

1. What are some of the problem's Bruce has with God? Which of these has a ring of familiarity for you?

2. Bruce complains that God is "ignoring me completely." Have you felt like this before? Share about a time recently when you felt like God was ignoring you.

Perhaps you can relate to David when he asked in Psalm 13:1-2, NIV:

How long, O LORD? Will you forget me forever? How long will you hide your face from me?
How long must I wrestle with my thoughts and every day have sorrow in my heart?
How long will my enemy triumph over me?

3. When something goes terribly wrong in your life, which of the following do you find the hardest to believe? Why do you think you struggle with that?

❏ God's existence   ❏ God's presence   ❏ God's goodness
❏ God's fairness   ❏ God's love   ❏ God's concern
❏ God's power   ❏ God's protection   ❏ God's plan

4. Bruce yells at God, "the gloves are off!" How do you think God feels about hearing our honest feelings even when they're pushy or accusatory?

OPENING PRAYER

God, sometimes when we pray, it feels as if the doors of Heaven are locked. So much of life makes no sense. Sometimes we want to run to You, and sometimes we want to run away. Father, please let us approach You with our conflicted, troubled hearts. We have no grand faith with which to impress you. Don't turn us away. Let us to sit with You, talk openly with You, and listen carefully to You.

OBJECTIVES FOR THIS SESSION

- Engage the spiritual issues that may intensify our depression
- Realize that many biblical characters struggled to understand God's ways
- Consider the response of Jesus to the big "Why?" questions
- Reassure group members He understands us even when we don't understand Him

While we most often recite the psalms of praise in our worship services, a significant number of the psalms contain laments, questions, complaints, protests, and desperate pleas for help. These should serve as a reassuring reminder that God can handle our raw emotions—in fact, He longs for this kind of gut-level, honest interaction.

DISCOVERING THE TRUTH – 35-40 MINUTES

LEADER: "Discovering the Truth" considers the stories of Gideon and Elijah. Read the text aloud or ask for volunteers. Keep things moving so you leave time for personal application in "Embracing the Truth" and "Connecting." Encourage the group as you note progress in "Refilling Our Tanks."

REFILLING OUR TANKS

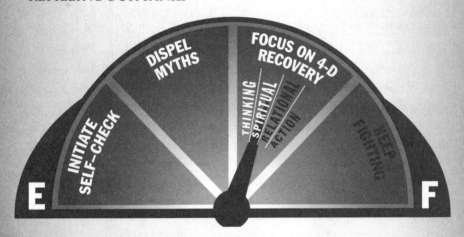

1. To which of the "cognitive distortions" in last week's assignment did realize that you were more susceptible? *All-or-Nothing Thinking ... Overgeneralization ... Mental Filter (dwell on negatives) ... Discounting the Positives (ignore positives) ... Jumping to Conclusions ... Magnification or Minimization ... Emotional Reasoning ... "Should" Statements ... Labeling ... Personalization or Blame.* What did you hear from God this week?

2. **On your own** to rate these statements according to the following scale: 0=Never; 1=Seldom; 2=Sometimes; 3=Often; 4=Always. Briefly discuss your 3s and 4s as a group.

   a. I feel empty. _____
   b. I'm not sure anymore what I care about or what I believe. _____
   c. I feel disconnected from the things that used to matter to me. _____
   d. I have trouble finding a sense of meaning or purpose in life. _____
   e. I don't believe God exists or I don't sense His presence at all. _____
   f. I doubt whether God really cares about me or about what's happening to me. _____
   g. I'm confused about God's purposes in permitting this season in my life. _____
   h. It's difficult for me to believe God has a positive plan for my life. _____

GIDEON'S STRUGGLE

¹ The Israelites did what was evil in the sight of the LORD. So the LORD handed them over to Midian seven years, ² and they oppressed Israel. Because of Midian, the Israelites made hiding places for themselves in the mountains, caves, and strongholds. ³ Whenever the Israelites planted crops, the Midianites, Amalekites, and the eastern peoples came and attacked them. ⁴ They encamped against them and destroyed the produce of the land, even as far as Gaza. They left nothing for Israel to eat, as well as no sheep, ox or donkey. ⁵ For the Midianites came with their cattle and their tents like a great swarm of locusts. They and their camels were without number, and they entered the land to waste it.

⁶ So Israel became poverty stricken because of Midian, and the Israelites cried out to the LORD. ⁷ When the Israelites cried out to Him because of Midian, ⁸ the LORD sent a prophet to them. He said to them, "This is what the LORD God of Israel says: 'I brought you out of Egypt and out of the place of slavery. ⁹ I delivered you from the power of Egypt and the power of all who oppressed you. I drove them out before you and gave you their land. ¹⁰ I said to you: I am the LORD your God. Do not fear the gods of the Amorites whose land you live in. But you did not obey Me.'"

¹¹ The Angel of the LORD came, and He sat under the oak that was in Ophrah, which belonged to Joash, the Abiezrite. His son Gideon was threshing wheat in the wine vat in order to hide it from the Midianites.

JUDGES 6:1-11, HCSB

3. With what problems did Israel struggle for seven long years because of the Midianites? How would you expect Gideon to respond to the Angel of the Lord?

¹² Then the Angel of the LORD appeared to him and said: "The LORD is with you, mighty warrior." ¹³ Gideon said to Him, "Please Sir, if the LORD is with us, why has all this happened? And where are all His wonders that our fathers told us about? They said, 'Hasn't the LORD brought us out of Egypt?' But now the LORD has abandoned us and handed us over to Midian."

JUDGES 6:12-13, HCSB

4. Why was Gideon feeling doubtful about God's concern for Israel?

5. Gideon's first question was "Why?". Describe a time when you've asked God "Why?" . How do you think God feels about our "Why?" questions?

6. God never answered the "Why?" question, but He eventually convinced Gideon of His presence, power, and promise. How can depressed emotions get in the way of realizing when God is trying to help us?

ELIJAH'S STRUGGLE

Recall in I Kings 18 that brave Elijah, with an amazing display of God's power, had victoriously taken on the prophets of the false god Baal. Then after Queen Jezebel threatened his life, Elijah folded up like a cheap lawn chair. He fled from Mount Carmel and collapsed more than a 100 miles away in Beers-heba in a dark depression.

4 [Elijah] sat down under a broom tree and prayed that he might die. He said, "I have had enough! LORD, take my life, for I'm no better than my fathers." 5 Then he lay down and slept under the broom tree. Suddenly, an angel touched him. The angel told him, "Get up and eat."

I KINGS 19:4-5, HCSB

7. How had Elijah's focus changed (verses 4-5) from the amazing time of victory on Mount Horeb? Tell about a time when pressure got to you and you essentially said to God, "I've had enough, Lord!"

We find another clue to Elijah's spiritually-driven depression in a statement Elijah made in I Kings 19:10 and then repeated in verse 14 in case God didn't catch it the first time:

13 Suddenly, [God's] voice came to him and said, "What are you doing here, Elijah?" 14 "I have been very zealous for the LORD God of Hosts," he replied, "but the Israelites have abandoned Your covenant, torn down Your altars, and killed Your prophets with the sword. I alone am left, and they're looking for me to take my life." 15 Then the LORD said to him, "Go and return by the way you came to the Wilderness of Damascus. ... 18 But I will leave 7,000 in Israel—every knee that has not bowed to Baal and every mouth that has not kissed him."

I KINGS 19:13-18, HCSB

Elijah really believed he was the only prophet of God left. He had told the prophets of Baal as much when he challenged them: "*I am the only one of the LORD's prophets left*" (1 Kings 18:22). Elijah had fallen into a deep rut; God' solution was to correct his faulty thinking and direct him to climb back onto the path.

8. What do you think happened within and around Elijah that caused him to lose his God-centered perspective after the major victory in 1 Kings 18? Tell about a time when you worked so hard and long on something that you lost perspective to the point you became discouraged, thinking you were the only one who cared what happened.

9. God surprised Elijah with this information: "*I will leave 7,000 in Israel—every knee that has not bowed to Baal and every mouth that has not kissed him.*" When you're depressed, what are the spiritual dangers of isolating yourself or concluding no one else cares?

10. When you're depressed, do you tend to draw people around you or isolate yourself? Who can you count on for support when you are at your lowest?

EMBRACING THE TRUTH – 25-30 MINUTES

JESUS AND THE WHY QUESTION

Many people in the Bible besides Gideon asked God "Why?". Job asked why God let him suffer after he had lived righteously (Job 13:24). The psalmist asked why the wicked prosper and the righteous suffer (Psalm 94:3-7). Jeremiah asked why God had sent him on a doomed prophetic mission (Jeremiah 20:14-18). Jesus' disciples asked why a man had been born blind (John 9:1-2). Some people in a crowd asked Jesus why God had let Pilate kill innocent Galileans and sprinkle their blood on his pagan sacrifices (Luke 13:1). After Jesus allowed Lazarus to die, Martha questioned Jesus' interest in her brother (John 11:21). The why question is one of our favorite questions, but God seldom answers it.

During one of His visits to Jerusalem, Jesus and His disciples encountered a blind man—perhaps a beggar they passed on the street every day.

¹ As [Jesus] went along, he saw a man blind from birth. His disciples asked him, ² "Rabbi, who sinned, this man or his parents, that he was born blind?" ³ "Neither this man nor his parents sinned," said Jesus, "but this happened so that the work of God might be displayed in his life"

JOHN 9:1-3, NIV

The Message paraphrased Jesus' answer this way: *"You're asking the wrong question. You're looking for someone to blame. There is no such cause-effect here. Look instead for what God can do."*

IMPORTANT NEWS FLASH: Jesus didn't look at tragedies in terms of cause and effect, but rather as opportunities to encounter God.

1. Why do you think we so often ask "Why?" as though we're looking for factual answers to cause and effect? In your opinion, would factual answers make tragedies easier to handle, unfair situations more manageable, or losses less devastating?

Typically, why questions are anguished cries from our battered hearts disguised as concerns of our intellects. In truth, we need a Comforter far more than we need an answer man.

2. How do you think someone goes about encountering God in a tragic or stress-filled situation?

3. How would encountering God in a tough times help you escape the crushing pressure of the bad situation? How might it help you move toward a positive solution to the bad situation?

4. How do you think meeting God in a difficult time would lessen the likelihood of becoming depressed because of it?

ON THE MAT WITH GOD

Many of us struggle with the concept of wrestling with God. And yet, most of us would like to pin Him down and hold Him until He provides us the answers we want and believe we deserve. Questions we crave to get answered include: "How long is the pain going to last?" ... "Why has this happened in my life?" ... "Where were You, God, and where are You now?" ... "What do you expect me to do now?" ... "How can I move on with my life now that this has happened?" ... "How can any good Father let this happen to His child?" The good news is that God invites us to wrestle with Him, because He knows it's a critical part of our healing process. **Let's see what we can learn from Jacob ...**

²⁴ *Jacob was left alone, and a man [God] wrestled with him until daybreak.* ²⁵ *When the man saw that He could not defeat him, He struck Jacob's hip as they wrestled and dislocated his hip socket.* ²⁶ *Then He said to Jacob, "Let Me go, for it is daybreak." But Jacob said, "I will not let You go unless You bless me."* ²⁷ *"What is your name?" the man asked. "Jacob!" he replied.* ²⁸ *"Your name will no longer be Jacob," He said. "It will be Israel because you have struggled with God and with men and have prevailed."* ²⁹ *Then Jacob asked Him, "Please tell me Your name." But He answered, "Why do you ask My name?" And He blessed him there.* ³⁰ *Jacob then named the place Peniel, "For," he said, "I have seen God face to face, and I have been delivered."* ³¹ *The sun shone on him as he passed by Penuel—limping on his hip.*

GENESIS 32:24-31, HCSB

5. According to verse 24, who was with Jacob when his wrestling match began? What might have been Jacob's motive for picking this fight ... what was he seeking (verse 26)?

6. We're never told what blessing Jacob wanted from God, but we know he walked away satisfied. What three blessings did God eventually give him? In your present situation, what do you want from God?

7. If God's goal was to defeat Jacob, He could have crushed him at any point. God let Jacob battle for an extended time until he was ready and able to receive the blessings God held for him. What role do you play in your journey through the desert of depression?

8. What's it worth to you to receive the blessings God gave Jacob: a new name (fresh start and identity); reconnection and intimacy with God; and "deliverance" from his pain? What keeps you from continuing to wrestle with God?

Connecting – 10-15 Minutes

> LEADER: Use this "Connecting" time to help group members become more real with God. Read aloud the "So How Do You Really Feel?" introduction. Then, show Scene 8, "Yelling at the Lord," from The Apostle, where Robert Duvall's character Sonny has a shouting prayer session with God (from 25:33 to 27:42 minutes on the DVD timer).

So How Do You Really Feel?

Many other godly people have joined Jacob in wrestling or challenging God. Robert Duvall starred as Pentecostal preacher Sonny Dewey in the film The Apostle. Sonny, while developing a thriving ministry and making a huge impact for God, also struggled with womanizing on the road. Eventually, his wife cheated on him, and he subsequently attacked a man in anger. Listen to the unique conversation Sonny initiates with God. It's quite similar to the conversation Job had with God, except that Job was fully righteous.

1. What do you think Sonny expected to accomplish by getting mad at God? What do you think about his approach to God?

Based on Sonny's "wrestling match" with God, he ended up setting out on his own for another location and planted another thriving church, helping to heal many wounded souls in the process. He did all this prior to being apprehended by law enforcement for his past crimes.

2. How did this path differ from Sonny's expectations during his yelling prayer? How was it better in the larger picture?

3. Why are we reluctant to talk this honestly with God? What barriers would we need to overcome to do so?

You can't unleash your raw emotions in most human relationships without becoming abusive, but God is big. You cannot injure Him. And He is secure enough to handle your outbursts without retaliating. One of Job's yelling prayers sounded like this ...

²⁰ Please, God, I have two requests; grant them so I'll know I count with you: ²¹ First, lay off the afflictions; the terror is too much for me. ²² Second, address me directly so I can answer you, or let me speak and then you answer me. ²³ How many sins have been charged against me? Show me the list—how bad is it? ²⁴ Why do you stay hidden and silent? Why treat me like I'm your enemy?

JOB 13:20-24, THE MESSAGE

Job would later apologize to God for those words and others like them (42:3), but look how God responds to Job after correcting his limited understanding of the Larger Story.

⁷ After GOD had finished addressing Job, he turned to Eliphaz the Temanite and said, "I've had it with you and your two friends. I'm fed up! You haven't been honest either with me or about me—not the way my friend Job has. ⁸ So here's what you must do. Take seven bulls and seven rams, and go to my friend Job. Sacrifice a burnt offering on your own behalf. My friend Job will pray for you, and I will accept his prayer. He will ask me not to treat you as you deserve for talking nonsense about me, and for not being honest with me, as he has."

JOB 42:7-8, THE MESSAGE

4. How did God respond to Job and then to his friends? How might your relationship with God change if you more fully accept the fact that God loves you, and loves to engage with you, especially in your messiness?

LEADER: *If your group is ready, invite them into a time of brutally honest prayer. This is a time to bring our authentic selves to God. It's not a time to shock other people nor to "outdo" someone else. Not everyone has to pray. Set the stage with your own heart-felt expression to God. Voice a brief closing prayer after all who wish to pray have done so. Before you close the meeting, ask people to share prayer and support needs that the group can remember throughout the coming week.*

MY PRAYER AND SUPPORT NEEDS:

MY GROUP'S PRAYER AND SUPPORT NEEDS:

TAKING IT HOME

LOOKING INWARD: A QUESTION TO TAKE TO MY HEART

After Jesus fed 5,000 people, He had a confrontation with Jewish leaders in which He claimed to be the "Bread of Life" (John 6:26-58). So many were confused by what Jesus said that a large part of His following deserted Him. Jesus turned to the Twelve and asked them point-blank if they wanted to leave too. Peter answered for the group in verses 68-69: *"Lord, who will we go to? You have the words of eternal life. We have come to believe and know that You are the Holy One of God!"*

The point isn't that Peter and the others understood Jesus' teaching better than those who left. The point is that they clung to their trust that He was "the Holy One of God" who would make their lives count—even if they didn't always know what He was up to.

* Consider events in your life that have been painful, hard to accept, and harder to understand. Imagine Jesus says, "A lot of people have given up and left over less than you've suffered. What about you? Are you still up for following Me? Why?"

LOOKING UPWARD: QUESTIONS TO TAKE TO GOD

* God, were You there when my life got turned upside down? What were You doing at that time? How did You feel about what happened?

* My Father, do You feel the emotions I'm feeling toward You? What is it that You and I need to wrestle to the ground?

LOOKING FORWARD: PREPARATION FOR SESSION SIX

Consider these questions to prepare for the group discussion in Session 6. Write your thoughts and feelings in the "Relationships Journal" on page 77 as you journey onward.

1. When I'm depressed, do I typically want to be with others or by myself? How do I think this preference affects the depth and length of my depression?

2. Who (individual or group) has stood by me during a difficult period in my past? What did I gain from those relationships? What did others gain from sticking with me?

3. Who could I call at 3 a.m. if I needed someone to talk to or come over just to be with me? With what kind of person would I be willing to be this vulnerable?

Relationships Journal

Incarnation

"OK, children; everybody hold hands and look both ways before you cross the street."

I think that's pretty good advice. I'm an only child, pretty self-sufficient, always have been—very sociable, but never really leaning on anybody. Besides, I'm a counselor. I'm strong so people can slump and prop themselves up on me. I've heard that doctors are lousy patients. I've been a patient of sorts for much of this year, and I have learned to welcome visitors. I've found the humility and courage to ask them to stay for a while, even inquire if they can come back tomorrow. I need them. Being an outgoing people helper, a class clown, a writer, a mentor to writers, an encourager, a calligrapher who surprises people with homemade, personalized birthday cards … I have a lot of fans.

However, depression has exposed my poverty and my need of deep friendships. I discovered that I had a few Garden of Gethsemane friends in the wings. I'll never forget Roger telling me, "This season does not define you nor does it alter our friendship." I remember Randy grabbing my hand and telling me with tears in his eyes, "Don't you leave me, buddy!" He said he needed me and that I had to stick around. I didn't know what I had to offer but I agreed to hang on. Roger, Randy, Doug, and Gwen kept the lifelines in the water.

My children treated me like I was a good and normal Dad, which is the best gift they could have given me. I felt like a very flawed husband, but my wife, Dorrie, battered down my walls of defeat and shame with unconditional love. She told me that I didn't need to be perfect, that for her and the boys, "pretty good is good enough."

I'm learning that the Incarnation continues to happen—the gift of people to me who are "Jesus with skin on."

FORGE HEALING RELATIONSHIPS:

SHARING THE LOAD

BREAKING THE ICE – 10-15 MINUTES

> LEADER: The "Breaking the Ice" questions for this session focus on the importance of supportive relationships. Encourage people to consider what they value in friends and have some fun in the process. Choose only two of these questions for the sake of time.

1. When you were a child, who was your best friend? What was it that made this relationship strong?

2. Which of the following activities would you least like to do completely alone? Which activities could you handle on your own?

On my own   No way

On my own	No way	
❏	❏	Scuba dive Australia's Great Barrier Reef
❏	❏	Make a speech to a crowd of 2,000
❏	❏	Teach a Sunday school class of 30 kindergartners for a year
❏	❏	Work the customer service desk at Wal-Mart on December 26 processing returns and refunds
❏	❏	Pack and move all my furniture and belongings to another home
❏	❏	Land an airplane safely with the help of the control tower after the pilot passed out
❏	❏	Travel in a foreign country where I've never been
❏	❏	Walk at midnight through an urban ghetto known for gang activity

3. If you could choose any mentor in the world to coach you for a year in any skill or subject, who would you choose and what would the area of interest be?

OPENING PRAYER

Dear God, thank You for this group. We've shared things we thought we never would, and we've found this to be a safe place. We wish we could take our group home, to work, and even to church. It's a powerful thing to be heard, understood, accepted, and supported. We're grateful that You don't expect us to make this journey alone. Thanks for the caring people You've sent into our lives at strategic times. Meet us here today and help us value of meaningful relationships in our lives.

OBJECTIVES FOR THIS SESSION

- Recognize that God doesn't expect us to make it through life's difficulties alone
- Realize five beneficial qualities of relationships
- Discover three categories of relationships everyone needs
- Welcome God's gift of relationships as a vital part of recovery from depression
- Continue to open up more in this group and in our other relationships

DISCOVERING THE TRUTH – 25-30 MINUTES

As we've grown comfortable as a group, there's a good chance our relationships are already affecting you in positive ways. Be encouraged by but what we've accomplished together as a group! As we continue refilling our tanks, we'll focus on the relational aspect.

REFILLING OUR TANKS

LEADER: ASK about any insights gained from homework questions related to relating to and to wrestling with God. In this session, "Discovering the Truth" is a little shorter and "Embracing the Truth" is a little longer than usual. Encourage some vulnerability by modeling openness about your struggles and experiences. Ask for volunteers to read the various explanations and Scriptures.

You've learned the vital importance of wrestling with God until He comes and personally addresses your issues and gives direction. Reaching out to God in total dependence is necessary if we're going to defeat the enemy of our souls and demolish the strongholds that fuel depression. But what happens when our arms get tired, or when we fall down, or when our burdens become too heavy? A community of wounded warriors is powerful.

POWER IN COMMUNITY

LEADER: Ask five group members to read Ecclesiastes 4:9-12, NLT aloud as indicated.

Reader 1: Two people are better off than one, for they can help each other succeed.

Reader 2: If one person falls, the other can reach out and help. But someone who falls alone is in real trouble.

Reader 3: Likewise, two people lying close together can keep each other warm. But how can one be warm alone?

Reader 4: A person standing alone can be attacked and defeated, but two can stand back-to-back and conquer.

Reader 5: Three are even better, for a triple-braided cord is not easily broken.

1. What quality of supportive friendships is stressed in each of the five portions of Ecclesiastes 4:9-12?

   a.

   b.

   c.

   d.

   e.

2. How does the line "If one person falls, the other can reach out and help. But someone who falls alone is in real trouble" apply to someone experiencing depression? What does it suggest about the role of this group?

3. If we choose to grieve alone, why are we more vulnerable when the enemy attacks? How might you get stuck or diverted in your healing journey if you choose to go it alone?

4. One of the greatest gifts people can give is the gift of their time and undivided attention. Tell about a time when an individual or a group helped pick you up as you were struggling through a difficult time.

RISK IN COMMUNITY

From the beginning of Genesis where God said, "*It is not good for the man to be alone*" (2:18), to the end of time where the those aligned with Jesus live in eternal harmony with one another and God (Revelation 21:1-3), it's clear that God intends us to live in supportive spiritual community. God neither expects nor equips us to go it alone.

Jesus didn't live or serve in isolation. Apart from His time on the cross, He never lived in isolation from the Father and the Holy Spirit. His disciples were His companions as well as His apprentices. One evening before He faced the cross, Jesus called His three closest friends to stand with Him.

[36] Then Jesus came with them to a place called Gethsemane, and He told the disciples, "Sit here while I go over there and pray." [37] Taking along Peter and the two sons of Zebedee, He began to be sorrowful and deeply distressed. [38] Then He said to them, "My soul is swallowed up in sorrow—to the point of death. Remain here and stay awake with Me." [39] Going a little farther, He fell facedown and prayed, "My Father! If it is possible, let this cup pass from Me. Yet not as I will, but as You will." [40] Then He came to the disciples and found them sleeping. He asked Peter. "So, couldn't you stay awake with Me one hour?

MATTHEW 26:36-40, HCSB

5. What was Jesus' emotional state in the garden? Why did He want friends around Him, especially His closest friends?

6. Name a "Garden friend" that you could ask for help in the middle of the night. How does a person develop friendships like that? What are some of the things that keep us from developing deeper friendships?

7. What risks did Jesus take in making Himself so vulnerable to His friends? The guys let Jesus down ... big time! What are some other risks required to develop close, healing friendships?

Openness and honesty are vital if we're going to help each other to heal, tear down strongholds, replace lies with truth, and find joy in the midst of life's stresses. Openness requires risk and vulnerability, but if we treat each other as unique and valuable members of the same body, we'll find new strength.

EMBRACING THE TRUTH – 40-45 MINUTES

TYPES OF CONNECTIONS AND FRIENDSHIPS YOU NEED

Different friendships play different roles in our lives. We can't expect one friend to meet every kind of relational need. People who expect this drive potential friends away. Such people are perceived as too needy, demanding, and draining. We need many friends, and we need to let each of them provide the kind of support they can. **Let's look at three types of friendships.**

TYPE 1: Understanding and Supportive Friendships

Be completely humble and gentle; be patient, bearing with one another in love.

EPHESIANS 4:2, NIV

¹² As God's chosen people, holy and dearly loved, clothe yourselves with compassion, kindness, humility, gentleness and patience. ¹³ Bear with each other and forgive whatever grievances you may have against one another. Forgive as the Lord forgave you.

COLOSSIANS 3:12-13, NIV

1. What traits for healthy, healing friendships stand out to you in Ephesians 4:2 and Colossians 3:12-14? Discuss friendships you have in which these traits are evident and where you're free to be yourself?

2. Both passages call on Christ-followers to "bear with" one another. That means to "put up with" one another. Who in your extended family is a little odd or demanding so that you have to "bear with" him or her? What makes this person challenging to love or enjoy being around?

Sometimes in families (relatives or spiritual families) we put up with quirks, unique personalities, and strange behavior because "they're family." When we suffer from depression, we probably aren't at our charming best either. We need people who will "bear with us in love."

Praise be to ... the Father of compassion and the God of all comfort, who comforts us in all our troubles, so that we can comfort those in any trouble with the comfort we ourselves have received from God.

2 CORINTHIANS 1:3-4, NIV

3. Who among your circle of friends is willing to "put up with" your quirks in order to give you comfort? In what ways could you let that person know how important he or she is to you?

Dietrich Bonhoeffer spoke of a healthy balance in friendships: "Let him who avoids community beware of solitude. Let him who avoids solitude beware of community." Counselors use the term "codependent" to refer to people who, in an attempt to find significance, security, and self-worth, live based on a pattern of excessive and painful dependency on compulsive behaviors and especially on approval from others.

4. Draw an X on the line to identify where you find yourself in relating to others in general. Put another X to identify how you relate to your closest friends. Are there any concerns or struggles you'd like to share with the group?

Isolated   Connected &   Codependent
                           Interdependent

TYPE 2: Challenging and Inspiring Friendships

While we need friends who "mourn with those who mourn" (Romans 12:15) and support us, we also need friends who challenge us, push us, urge us, hold us accountable, and even confront us when necessary.

⁶ Wounds from a friend can be trusted. But an enemy multiplies kisses ... ¹⁷ As iron sharpens iron, so one man sharpens another.

PROVERBS 27:6,17, NIV

5. Who in your circle of friends is most likely to challenge your thinking or confront your behavior? Who is most likely to tell you the truth even when it's hard to say or hear?

6. How are you likely to respond to a friend who dares to challenge or inspire you?

TYPE 3: Entertaining and Energizing Friendships

Nobody needs a constant stream of serious friends supporting or challenging him or her. Most of the time we need friends who are just fun. Maybe our entertaining and energizing friends also have the ability to support or challenge us, but maybe they don't. Some of our friends are simply friends who make our lives pleasant.

7. What kinds of things that refresh your life do you enjoy doing with your friends?

In return, you need to be the kind of friend who entertains and energizes those around you. Jesus said, *"Love your neighbor as yourself"* (Mark 12:31). We need to balance the giving and taking in our friendships so we meet the needs of our friends as well as find our needs met through them. The Apostle Paul had this sort of thing in mind when he told the Philippian Christians, *"Look not only to your own interests, but also to the interests of others"* (Philippians 2:4).

8. Henri Nouwen said that we are all wounded healers. Even when we are depressed, we need to be concerned about the welfare of our friends. How can caring for someone else improves our mood and refocus our thinking?

9. Tell about a time when you acted as an understanding and supportive friend to one of your friends who needed you. How did you feel after you helped your friend?

CAUTION: Obviously, those with a caregiver personality and gifts have to be careful. Caregivers have to set some limits of emotional availability to others in need so they don't neglect or avoid their own issues and care. Again, the key is balance. But many will testify that in the midst of depression doing something helpful or caring for someone else actually helps improve our mood and takes our negative focus off our own condition.

CONNECTING – 15-20 MINUTES

LEADER INSTRUCTIONS FOR THE GROUP EXPERIENCE: Have a group member read James 5:16-18 aloud. Then pass out three small index cards to each person. Instruct them to take about 10 minutes on their own to write on each card as indicated. When you pull the group back together, instruct people to pass their card sets to the next person of the same gender on their right.

Tapping into the Power of Community

James, the brother of Jesus, knew that we all have failures, issues, and regrets, and that we all need help to get through life. James gives us encouragement and one vital key to making it through the "ups" and especially the "downs" of life.

¹⁶ Confess your sins to each other and pray for each other so that you may be healed. The earnest prayer of a righteous person has great power and produces wonderful results. ¹⁷ Elijah was as human as we are, and yet when he prayed earnestly that no rain would fall, none fell for three and a half years! ¹⁸ Then, when he prayed again, the sky sent down rain and the earth began to yield its crops.

JAMES 5:16-18, NLT

As instructed by your group leader, take a few minutes **on your own** to jot a note on each of the index cards as indicated. Remember, there are risks in being vulnerable, but the upside potential is great.

On Card 1: List a burden, failure, issue, or regret you've been carrying on your own for which you'd appreciate support. Jot it down on the first card, write your name, and give a brief explanation.

On Card 2: List your biggest struggle in dealing with depression for which you'd appreciate support and prayer. Jot it down on the second card, write your name, and give a brief explanation.

On Card 3: What is it that someone could do outside these meetings to be encouraging to you as a friend? Think about the three different types of support we discussed. Jot it down on the third card, write your name, and give a brief explanation.

When your leader draws you back together as a group, pass your set of three cards to the next person of the same gender at your right. **IT'S IMPORTANT** for both your healing and the healing of the person who passed you his or her cards that you commit to:

(1) pray for his or her needs listed on the cards and

(2) take a little time to actually do the thing that's on card 3 to encourage him or her.

How can this group help you to feel comfortable as we make efforts to reach out to each other this week? How can we pray for you today?

My Prayer and Support Needs:

My Group's Prayer and Support Needs:

Taking It Home

The following questions ask you to look into your heart and focus on your deepest feelings about yourself. Our behaviors are the best indicators of what we really believe deep down. Look into the underlying beliefs in your heart where your truest attitudes and motives live. (See Psalm 51:6.) Spend time reflecting, and don't settle for a quick answer. Be sure to capture your thoughts and feelings.

Looking Inward: Questions to Take to My Heart

❋ You may feel that your load is too heavy to carry right now. You're probably right. Take a few minutes to identify people who could or who are engaging with you in *each* friendship category.

Understanding and Supportive Friendships:

_____

_____

Challenging and Inspiring Friendships:

_____

_____

Entertaining and Energizing Friendships:

_____

_____

❋ How do I feel in my innermost being that people will react if they know me as I truly am? How does that shape the way I interact with friends?

Looking Upward: Questions to Take to God

✴ God, what do You want to tell me about the way I approach relationships that may actually hinder my recovery from depression?

✴ Is there anyone You want me to reach out to who needs and would respond to my encouragement?

Looking Forward: Preparation for Session Seven

Consider these questions to prepare for the discussion in Session 7. Capture your thoughts and feelings in the "Gearing Up Journal" on page 91 as you continue on your journey.

1. In what physical exercise or activities do I currently engage?

2. What activity or hobby that I previously enjoyed have I stopped? Why?

3. How does depression affect my eating habits and sleeping pattern?

4. When in a depressive mood, we are susceptible to inactivity and isolation. When I'm depressed which of the following is most true?
   ❏ I have the energy of a slug on tranquilizers.
   ❏ My couch is like a magnet that keeps pulling me back.
   ❏ I don't enjoy my own company so I'm certain no one else will either.
   ❏ I'm grouchy and don't want to be around anybody.
   ❏ I make myself do productive things even if I don't feel like it.
   ❏ Other: _____

5. How willing am I to step back on the path God has laid out for me? How willing am I to keep wrestling with God—to stay engaged?

OPTIONAL: Watch either of these films this week and write down personal thoughts, feelings, and insights: *28 Days*, starring Sandra Bullock (2000) or *Stranger Than Fiction*, starring Will Ferrell and Maggie Gyllenhaal (2006).

Gearing Up Journal

Reemerging ... Again

I've had my Mount Carmel moments

when faith shackled Satan

on fireproofs altars and

mocked his flaming weakness;

when doubt was lightning-licked

from the trenches,

and trust wore a laurel wreath.

But the Jezebels have met me often in victory lane,

to watch sundown's pinnacle faith

retreating, coasting downhill

on training wheels,

pumping the breaks throughout the slope.

Finally I bury myself and my wheels in a cave—

a place of security only in my imagining.

I might never emerge and retake the mountain

save that still small voice from above

that ever beckons me to remount.

GET BACK IN THE ACTION:

GETTING OFF THE COUCH

BREAKING THE ICE – 10-15 MINUTES

> LEADER: *By now your group should be connecting well and supporting each other toward healing and wholeness. Even though the group is now used to deeper discussions, start out with some lighthearted "Breaking the Ice" questions. You may choose to skip question 2 for the sake of time.*

1. Congratulations! Imagine you're the Grand Prize Winner of the (totally made up) *Hollywood Film Prop Sweepstakes.* You get to own any prop ever used in any Hollywood film. (The only restriction is that it must be something that will fit in your house.) What prop do you choose? What movie is it from? What's the object's significance for you?

2. What is your favorite movie or book of all time? What is it that you like so much?

3. Although this may not be the best time in your life to ask, what is it that makes your heart come alive, that gets your blood pumping (beside a hungry bear chasing you through the woods)? Tell why.

OPENING PRAYER

God of life and creation, we need Your activity and energy in our group to teach us how to take action against our depression. Give us insight. Help each of us to know what You want us to do. Give us wisdom so we don't try to do too much and end up discouraged. Encourage us so we dare to do all that You want us to. Holy Spirit, grow the fruit of self-discipline in us so we persevere to our benefit and Your glory.

OBJECTIVES FOR THIS SESSION

- Explore the importance of rest, nourishment, exercise, and play in dealing with depression
- Consider appropriate action steps to combat depression
- Evaluate how resistance to taking action steps occurs in our lives
- Begin to develop a plan of action

DISCOVERING THE TRUTH – 20-25 MINUTES

It's vital to gain insight, correct stinking thinking, and realign our hearts with God and others. Eventually, though, we have to start putting new strategies into practice. We have to do things that will help us handle our lives better. As we continue refilling our tanks, we'll focus on the getting back in the action.

REFILLING OUR TANKS

You've learned the vital importance of wrestling with God until He comes and personally addresses your issues and direction. Reaching out to God in total dependence is necessary if we're going to defeat the enemy of our souls and demolish the strongholds that fuel our depression. But what happens when our arms get tired, or when we fall down, or when our burdens become too heavy for us? A community of wounded warriors is powerful in its effect.

JUST GIT UP!

Often when we're depressed, we don't want to do anything. No matter how bad our emotional inertia may be, it comes time to "just git up and git 'er done."

We've looked a couple of times at Elijah's depressive episode following his emotionally draining victory over the prophets of Baal in 1 Kings 18. Today we're going to visit that episode again and examine some of the physical factors that God addressed in helping His prophet recover and move on

Reader 1: *1 Kings 19:1-4*

Reader 2: *1 Kings 19:5-8*

Reader 3: *1 Kings 19:9-12*

Reader 4: *1 Kings 19:13-18*

1. Notice that after Elijah voiced his "I wish I could die" prayer, he fell asleep (verses 4-5). Why do you suppose Elijah wanted to sleep – how many possible reasons can you imagine? Why do you suppose God let Elijah sleep instead of bawling him out?

2. What do you think God was doing when he let Elijah nap and eat, nap and eat (verses 5-7)? God, who had sent fire down from the skies on Mount Carmel, certainly had the power to restore Elijah instantly. Why was the only miracle God performed here sending an angel who could cook?

3. Why do you suppose the Lord made Elijah explain to Him why he had run so far and so fast to get away from Jezebel (verses 10, 14)? What do you gain from hearing yourself say out loud things you've been rehearsing inside your head for a while?

4. Elijah had already seen God reveal Himself spectacularly in fire on Mount Carmel (1 Kings 18:38). Why do you suppose the Lord felt it was important to come to Elijah in a "gentle whisper" to address his depression (19:12-13)?

Let's review some of the practical interventions that composed God's "treatment plan" for Elijah:

- Rest
- Nutrition (food and liquids)
- Exercise (a bit extreme in this case)
- An assignment to complete

5. What would the result of Elijah's assignment be (verses 15-18)? How would accomplishing all this counteract his depression?

Embracing the Truth – 40-45 Minutes

We can use Elijah's experience as the starting point for evaluating how we need to act in order to deal with the causes and symptoms of depression in our lives. As we'll see, one of the big challenges in all this is keeping our balance. When we're depressed, we tend to swing to emotional and behavioral extremes. Healthy living often lies between the extremes.

Medications Are Not Sinful

Especially in our high stress, fast food, chemically filled world, depression can and often does have a strong medical component. Be sure to address any of the physical factors of depression listed in Session One. If you suffer from depression, you should have a thorough examination by your family doctor, and perhaps also by a psychiatric specialist, so you'll know if there are physical factors involved.

Rest or Run?

In the depth of his depression, Elijah needed big doses of physical exertion and complete rest. Our bodies always need both exercise and rest, but when we're depressed, the need becomes heightened. If we, like Elijah, Have been pushing too hard or for too long, rest is a vital need.

Then, because so many people were coming and going that they did not even have a chance to eat, [Jesus] said to them, "Come with me by yourselves to a quiet place and get some rest."

EPHESIANS 4:2, NIV

1. How can you tell the difference between fatigue caused by lethargy and fatigue caused by exertion? How will you know if you need exercise or a nap?

People who work hard sleep well, whether they eat little or much. But the rich seldom get a good night's sleep.

ECCLESIASTES 5:12, NLT

2. According to Ecclesiastes 5:12, what's the relationship between work or exercise and sleep? How has your depression been affected by your sleep and vice versa?

Depressed people seldom want to exercise. At the same time, we feel fatigue that is typically emotional rather than physical. This "fatigue" is caused by lethargy rather than exertion. Rest doesn't affect it. When you feel lethargic, don't give in to your emotions. Give your body a workout. Then give it rest.

3. What are you currently doing that could qualify as exercise? If needed, what changes could you make to your routine to incorporate more physical activity?

Exercise with a group or class has two added benefits:

- Being with people reduces any isolation and loneliness you may be experiencing.
- There will be less "cheating" and fewer "no-shows" in your exercise plan when you know that other people are expecting you. The encouragement and accountability are pluses!

4. Here are some individual and group exercise possibilities. The more you enjoy an activity, the more likely you will be to stick with it. Mix up your routines to add variety. Check the activities you would like to work into your schedule.

❏ Walking	❏ Hiking	❏ Cycling	❏ Swimming
❏ Running	❏ Tennis	❏ Golf	❏ Softball
❏ Basketball	❏ Bowling	❏ Karate	❏ Aerobics class
❏ Roller skating	❏ Pilates	❏ Tai Chi	❏ Dancing
❏ Jazzercise	❏ Jumping rope	❏ Weight training	
❏ Canoeing	❏ Other: _____		

Feast or Famine?

For the drunkard and the glutton will become poor, and grogginess will clothe them in rags.

PROVERBS 23:21, HCSB

Depression almost always impacts our appetite. Either we eat more, which is frequently called "emotional eating," or we have no appetite for food. Depression can lead either to weight gain or weight loss, along with the health issues that can accompany either of these conditions.

5. Just as alcohol is the "drug of choice" for some, food is the "drug of choice" for others. What are some of your favorite comfort foods? How does "emotional eating" backfire on you?

6. How do you think people who crave comfort foods can overcome those urges? How can people with no appetite get themselves to eat enough?

For those who don't eat well, God is as interested for His children to be satisfied with food as with sleep.

You [Lord] serve me a six-course dinner right in front of my enemies. You revive my drooping head; my cup brims with blessing.

PSALM 23:5, THE MESSAGE

Time to Play

We all need physical exercise to tone our muscles and give us a more positive outlook on life. Experts also recommend an additional low-impact group activity just for fun. That activity might be a hobby or craft, an educational or creative venture, or any other kind of recreation. The point is that most adults, especially depressed adults, forget how to play.

Here is a random sampling of "play" activities:

a. A sporting event	h. Movies	o. Cooking	v. Photography
b. Creative writing	i. Book club	p. Music lessons	w. Scrapbooking
c. Card-making class	j. Dancing	q. Calligraphy	x. Blog writing
d. A college class	k. Concerts	r. Live theater	y. Landscaping
e. An art course	l. Woodworking	s. Jewelry making	z. Collecting
f. Volunteer work	m. Political activism	t. Gardening	
g. Floral design	n. Gardening	u. A computer class	

7. Why do we tend to get away from activities—even interesting ones—and end up watching television?

8. What does it take to incorporate a new activity—even a beneficial one—into our already busy schedules?

RESISTING RESISTANCE

In applying any of the proactive strategies in this and previous sessions, you will encounter the Dragon of Resistance. The Dragon of Resistance is not a fire-breather that scorches those who come near his castle. This dragon guards the Gate of Action. His imposing presence partially blocks the gate, but it's his voice that keeps us from getting past him.

9. What are some of the things that the Dragon of Resistance will likely tell you when you try to implement even small positive changes?

10. How will the Dragon of Resistance try to keep you inactive and isolated? What do you think makes Resistance and Procrastination such compatible friends?

The Dragon of Resistance operates by *mocking* you and *hypnotizing* you. Resistance mocks you by telling you none of your actions will make any difference. Resistance hypnotizes you by luring you into further inactivity: "Your eyes are getting heavy." "You have no energy." "You need another nap." "Just one more show."

11. How should we respond when the Dragon of Resistance *mocks* our efforts to change? How should we respond to the "lullaby" of the Dragon meant to *hypnotize* us into further inaction?

CONNECTING – 20-25 MINUTES

LEADER INSTRUCTIONS FOR THE GROUP EXPERIENCE: You will need to bring a 10-pound (5 kg) dumbbell to the group. You may want to bring a lighter (5-pound or 2 kg) and a heavier weight, depending on the body types and strength levels of group members.

Pass around the weight(s) and invite members to do a few repetitions of bicep curls or overhead presses. Have each group member continue until they feel a strain on their muscles.

After all group members have taken turns doing repetitions with a weight, say something like, "The reason that weight training works in building muscle is that the weight creates resistance for the muscle. For example, when bending your arm while holding the weight, your muscle has to exert itself more than it would without the weight. The exertion created by the weight tears the smallest muscle fibers. The muscle fibers quickly repair themselves into larger, stronger ones. This tearing and repairing partially explains why your muscles ache after strenuous exercise."

1. Why would anyone engage in exercise that makes his or her muscles hurt? What does that have to do with pursuing an action plan to combat depression?

2. Do you find it easier to maintain an exercise regimen on your own or with the help of others going through the same discipline? Why?

3. How can we in this group support each other to deal with the Dragon of Resistance when he mocks or tries to hypnotize?

4. What are ways we can be more available to one another for support between sessions and even after the group completes this study?

5. If depression is not just a "head thing" but is impacted by my body, my movement, my activities, what adjustments do I need to make so my body can help my head? What is one positive thing I can do today? What three positive things can I do this week?

My Prayer and Support Needs:

My Group's Prayer and Support Needs:

Taking It Home

LOOKING INWARD: A QUESTION TO TAKE TO MY HEART

Look into your heart for the answer to this question. Don't worry about what you *ought* to feel. Look for the values, hopes, fears, and longings that motivate your most basic thoughts and actions. Every action has a corresponding belief that drives it. Try to be honest about what you believe in the deep recesses of your heart about God, yourself, and the world in which you live.

* When I give up on an action plan, what kind of trigger event am I usually responding to? What keeps me from responding in a better, more productive way?

LOOKING UPWARD: QUESTIONS TO TAKE TO GOD

* Father, what do I need to understand about You, or about me, about the Dragon of Resistance, or about life so I can sense Your presence and power during my darkest hours?

LOOKING FORWARD: PREPARATION FOR SESSION EIGHT

Consider these questions to prepare you for the group discussion in the final session. Capture your thoughts and feelings in the "Overcoming Journal" on page XX as you continue on your journey.

1. Why do you suppose God doesn't heal most people of depression (or cancer, etc.) in the instantaneous manner in which Jesus healed people of various afflictions during His days on earth?

2. Jesus said, "I came so they can have real and eternal life, more and better life than they ever dreamed of." (John 10:10, The Message). He also said, "You will have suffering in this world. Be courageous! I have conquered the world." (John 16:33). How can fullness of life, peace, and troubles go together?

3. What do you think it means for God's grace to be "sufficient" for all of our weaknesses (2 Corinthians 12:9)?

4. How much do you think your victories *in spite of* depression or your triumphs over depression depend on your efforts? How much depends on God?

5. How can a Christ-follower who suffers depression still glorify God?

OVERCOMING JOURNAL

My Tour de France. My Iwo Jima. My Jordan

I never cared about the Tour de France until Lance Armstrong began
winning the grueling 2,241mile, 3-week race after surviving cancer.
I wore a yellow wristband and bought a 10/2 cap. October 2 was the date that
Lance was diagnosed with cancer.

I know what it is to have a date that you want to defeat.
A date that changes you but you refuse to let it define you or finish you.
A date you resist and stiff-arm. An anniversary that you intend
to celebrate by jamming your flag in the ground atop the recaptured island
like the soldiers at Iwo Jima. A monument that is not a tombstone marking the
place of your demise, but an altar of triumph and thanksgiving.

After the Israelites crossed the Jordan, Joshua instructed them to erect
the "stones of remembrance." They were survivors, victors.
The desert was behind them. God had delivered them after a grueling journey.
I'm a survivor, a victor too. I'm dancing on the banks of my Jordan.

I'm dancing with a limp ...
but I'm dancing all the same!

LEAPING WITH A LIMP:

STAYING IN THE FIGHT TO BEAT DEPRESSION

BREAKING THE ICE – 10-15 MINUTES

LEADER: You may want to allow even more personal sharing in this final session. Group members now have the map for the journey to healing, but the journey has really only begun. Be sensitive to the need for closure as well as continued support. Choose two of the "Breaking the Ice" questions.

OPTIONAL MOVIE NIGHT: Since the movie The Legend of Bagger Vance *plays a key role in Session 8, we would encourage you to set up an additional meeting to watch the film together and be prepared to discuss recovering your "authentic swing."*

1. Tell about a childhood accident in which you broke a bone or sprained a joint. How clumsy were you during the recovery period? Who signed your cast?

2. As an adult, what has been your worst experience with walking on crutches or otherwise being hobbled by a bad foot, ankle, or leg?

3. What's the most embarrassing stumble or fall you've ever taken?

Opening Prayer

God, thank You for this Beyond the Shadows *study and especially this group of people. It's been good to be together and share our stories with friends we trust. We've tried to examine the way we think. And we've tried to hear from You. Thanks for speaking peace and truth into our chaos.*

Just now we laughed about broken bones. Our "broken" emotions aren't so funny. Hearts don't heal the same way arms and legs do. Meet us in this session. Let us leave here with confidence that You are healing us from the inside out. We are not cripples. We may "walk" with a limp just as Jacob after his deeply personal encounter with You, but we're walking nonetheless.

Objectives for this Session

- Accept the often-incomplete and ongoing nature of healing from depression
- Embrace the ongoing tension between John 10:10 and John 16:33
- Learn to address the wounds of the past by embracing our pain and rejecting our shame
- Accept the gift of God's grace as He continues to heal our depression
- Choose to trust, worship, and serve Christ in favorable and unfavorable circumstances

DISCOVERING THE TRUTH – 35-40 MINUTES

LEADER: ASK about any insights this week related to the Dragon of Resistance.
We're going to look at two Bible stories about people who needed healing and how God brought His grace to bear on their lives. In the first instance, God's grace led to physical healing. In the second, it didn't. There are lessons for us in both situations. Try to keep things moving.

Wow! This is the final session of our *Beyond the Shadows* group. We've made great progress together, but note that the final step in our process is to "keep fighting." Battling depression is not a one-time event for most people. God will take us on an amazing journey through and beyond our shadows if we just stay engaged and do not lose heart!

In this session, we want to think about realistic expectations for recovery from depression. We differ from one another in so many ways. It shouldn't be surprising that we will also differ in how we recover.

UNEXPECTED GRACE

The Apostle Paul was no doubt the greatest church planter in history. God used him in great ways and yet he carried the burden of a chronic infirmity or disability. Let's consider how God responded to Paul's crying out for healing.

[7] So to keep me from becoming proud, I was given a thorn in my flesh, a messenger from Satan to torment me and keep me from becoming proud. [8] Three different times I begged the Lord to take it away. [9] Each time he said, "My grace is all you need. My power works best in weakness." So now I am glad to boast about my weaknesses, so that the power of Christ can work through me. [10] That's why I take pleasure in my weaknesses, and in the insults, hardships, persecutions, and troubles that I suffer for Christ. For when I am weak, then I am strong.

2 CORINTHIANS 12:7-10, NLT

1. Paul attributed his "thorn in the flesh" to Satan. Why do you think the enemy attacks us when we are deepening our personal spiritual lives or making strides for the Kingdom of God?

2. Like all those who understood that God is the ultimate Ruler and Healer, Paul "begged" God to take away his suffering. Psalm 72:12 says, "For [God] will deliver the needy who cry out, the afflicted who have no one to help" (NIV). Why is it that throughout the Scriptures, we're told of the importance of crying out to God?

3. God refused to heal Paul and remove his suffering. Paul gives one reason for this in verse 7. As you think about the Larger Story of redemption and also about Paul's personal life and ministry, what other reasons might explain God's surprising response to Paul?

4. What do you think God was promising Paul when He said, "My grace is all you need" (verse 9)? How do God's power and our weakness interact to honor Him and satisfy us?

GRACE WITH HEALING

LEADER: *Before the session, recruit four group members to read portions of Acts 3:1-10 aloud to open this discussion.*

Acts 3 opens with the first story of a miraculous healing by Jesus' disciples after His return to Heaven. Instead of focusing on that theological fact, let's try to imagine what the healing experience was like for this poor, unsuspecting, disabled beggar who was hoping to make enough money to get through another day.

Reader 1: Acts 3:1-3

Reader 2: Acts 3:4-6

Reader 3: Acts 3:7-8

Reader 4: Acts 3:9-10

This man had never walked a day in his life (Acts 3:2). His highest hope when Peter and John stopped to talk to him was that they might give him a decent donation (verse 4).

5. What kinds of thoughts might have passed through this man's mind when Peter said, "I have neither silver nor gold, but what I have, I give to you: In the name of Jesus Christ the Nazarene, get up and walk!" (verse 6)?

6. This hurting man didn't know Peter, but he'd obviously heard of Jesus. What would have happened if he had just continued to lie there without crying out? What would have happened without trusting Jesus or reaching up for the hand extended to him?

7. In addition to skeletal and neurological defects, the muscles of this man's legs would have been badly atrophied. When the text says, "at once his feet and ankles became strong" (verse 7), how many different kinds of miracles were occurring physically, emotionally, spiritually, and relationally?

8. What mix of emotions do you imagine motivated the man to jump about and shout praises to God in the stately, solemn confines of the Temple (verse 8)? How did people in the temple area react to the antics of the healed man (verses 9-10)?

9. How were God's grace and power effective in both Paul's lack of healing and in the lame man's healing? What can we learn from this?

EMBRACING THE TRUTH – 30-35 MINUTES

FACING OUR SHADOWS

As we noted at the start of this group, an eight-session study is not "the cure" for depression. Our goal has been to be used by God as a catalyst for each person's healing and growth. Without a doubt, we will each find ourselves again in the shadows unable to see the light, but we now have some powerful spiritual weapons and friends whom we can call. Let's study one last story.

Director Robert Redford explains *The Legend of Bagger Vance* is a film "about a man who's lost his authentic swing." He describes the journey of a man "who falls into darkness through some disconnect with his soul, and then of his coming back into the light with the help of a spiritual guide." In Junuh's (Matt Damon) story, the disconnect happened during traumatic events in combat when men under his leadership were slaughtered. Finding his authentic golf swing is symbolic of rediscovering and redeeming his life.

> *LEADER INSTRUCTIONS FOR THE GROUP EXPERIENCE: Have a TV/DVD player set up. Read the preceding introduction to set up the story, and then show a scene from the 2000 film,* The Legend of Bagger Vance, *starring Will Smith, Matt Damon, and Charlize Theron. Show part of Scene 29 "The Drop" (begin about 4 minutes in at 1:37:08 and continue to end of Scene 29 at 1:43:35 on the DVD timer). After showing the clip, discuss the following questions.*

1. Alone in the woods, the full force of Junuh's trauma came flooding back. What do you think was going through his mind? Discuss the various intense feelings he displayed.

2. When he entered the woods, Junuh's focus was on the darkness that surrounded him rather than on the light—the way out. He was ready to give up in despair and shame. According to Lamentations 3:17-20, what are some lies that become deeply embedded into the wounds in our hearts and can lead us to despair?

[Jeremiah shares his true feelings in a difficult time:] ¹⁷ *I gave up on life altogether. I've forgotten what the good life is like.* ¹⁸ *I said to myself, "This is it. I'm finished. God is a lost cause."* ¹⁹ *I'll never forget the trouble, the utter lostness, the taste of ashes, the poison I've swallowed.* ²⁰ *I remember it all—oh, how well I remember—the feeling of hitting the bottom.*

LAMENTATIONS 3:17-20, THE MESSAGE

3. What key truth did Bagger reveal to Junuh about his burden and what he needed to do with it? How does this correspond to Jesus' promise in Matthew 5:4, and why is remembering and grieving our losses so vital in healing from depression?

Blessed are those who mourn, because they will be comforted.   MATTHEW 5:4, HCSB

4. What critical formula for healing (that we often get backwards) does Jesus model for us in Hebrews 12:2?

... keeping our eyes on Jesus, the source and perfecter of our faith, who for the joy that lay before Him endured a cross and despised the shame, and has sat down at the right hand of God's throne.

HEBREWS 12:2, HCSB (EMPHASIS ADDED)

Bagger says, "Ain't a soul on this earth ain't got a burden to carry he don't understand." Like many of us, Junuh allowed his wounds, his failures, his burden, to define him. We try to escape rather than remembering our wounds and staying in our pain until we figure out the path to "find our swing." Unwilling to face our intense emotions or to take responsibility about where we go from here, we let our burdens become our identity, we accept lies about ourselves and God, and we settle for survival in place of real life.

**The battle Junuh waged in the shadows is the same one we each fight—
the battle for our hearts and the legacy of our lives.**

³ *For though we live in the world, we do not wage war as the world does.* ⁴ *The weapons we fight with are not the weapons of the world. On the contrary, they have divine power to demolish strongholds.* ⁵ *We demolish arguments and every pretension that sets itself up against the knowledge of God, and we take captive every thought to make it obedient to Christ.*

2 CORINTHIANS 10:3-5, NIV

5. In 2 Corinthians 10:4-5, Paul talks about demolishing "strongholds." When you imagine castles and fortified strongholds, what does it take to demolish them? Using this illustration, what kind of battle and reconstruction process would you envision for demolishing the lies and deceiving voices that hold us captive?

When Junuh struggled to remember his pain and his authentic swing, Bagger gave incredible assurance in the same way God speaks to us: "You ain't alone. I'm right here with you. I've been here all along."

¹ Do not be afraid, for I have ransomed you. I have called you by name; you are mine. ² When you go through deep waters, I will be with you. When you go through rivers of difficulty, you will not drown. When you walk through the fire of oppression, you will not be burned up; the flames will not consume you. ³ For I am the LORD, your God, the Holy One of Israel, your Savior.

ISAIAH 43:1B-3A, NLT

Fear is often the greatest enemy to meaningful life change. We long to return to what's familiar rather than take risks and face the fear of the unknown.

6. What assurances does God give in Isaiah 43:1-3 for the various fears we might face? Which of these assurances gives you the greatest comfort? Explain.

FIGHTING YOUR WAY OUT

It must have felt strange to the man Peter healed in Acts 3 to have control over limbs he had never used. He tried them out with the enthusiasm of a child in a celebratory romp through the Temple court. In the days that followed he must have made discovery after discovery about what healthy legs could do. He also faced new responsibilities. He couldn't beg any more. He needed to find employment and take on tasks he hadn't been able to handle previously. His new abilities exposed him to both greater opportunities and greater responsibilities.

7. Why do you suppose God doesn't usually heal us instantaneously from depression? How does God use a group like this to move us through stages of recovery from depression?

8. Dr. Alison Evans says, *"You don't just gracefully walk out of depression; you fight your way out."* What do you suppose is the proper balance between resting in God's grace and power and actively working to overcome depression?

CONNECTING – 15-20 MINUTES

LEADER Use this final "Connecting" to launch group members as they continue on the healing journey. Make yourself and other group leaders available for ongoing support. Look for ways the group members can continue to support one another. Be sure to celebrate each person's progress!

FULL LIFE IN A TROUBLED WORLD

1. Jesus said, *"I have come that they might have life and have it in abundance"* (John 10:10, HCSB). In what sense can you say that your life is full? In what sense do you feel you're missing the abundance of life Jesus promised?

2. Jesus also said, *"I have told you all this so that you may have peace in me. Here on earth you will have many trials and sorrows. But take heart, because I have overcome the world"* (John 16:33, NLT). How is it possible to have peace in a world characterized by trials and sorrows?

LEADER: Write "Life ... Joy ... Peace. John 10:10" *on one large flat stone.*
Write "Trouble ... Pain ... Sorrow. John 16:33" *on another to illustrate the idea that we must accept both joy/peace and pain/suffering coexisting in this life. Pass the stones around the group so each member holds them. You might want to create a set of stones for each group member to take home as a reminder.*

The concepts of John 10:10 and John 16:33—a full life and a troubled life—may seem contradictory, but they are both true. Imagine John 10:10 and John 16:33 inscribed on two stones. Living the Christian life means forever holding John 10:10 in one hand and John 16:33 in the other.

3. Author Lewis Smedes wrote that "true joy must somehow be compatible with human pain" and "only the heart that hurts has the right to true joy." What has depression taught you about the nature of true joy?

GROUP REFLECTION AND ENCOURAGEMENT

This is our last opportunity during this study to share our hearts with one another. Let's look back over the course of these eight sessions and reflect on what we've learned and what God has done during this time.

4. Look at the other group members. How have you seen specific people make progress through this *Beyond the Shadows* process? How have you experienced encouragement from others in this group?

5. At a personal level, what's one of the most important things you need to remember in the future when you feel depression coming on? What's the most important lesson you've learned about the value of group support in your struggle against depression?

Take turns around the circle completing the first question and then go around again for the second:

- I feel I'm getting stronger because ...

- I want to thank all of you for ...

Metaphorically speaking, each group member's ankles and feet have been strengthened in varying degrees through this group, but we all will probably walk with a limp ... just as God intends. His "power works best in weakness."

GROUP NEXT STEPS

At the end of this Beyond the Shadows *experience, group members will feel a close sense of connection. At the same time, they're aware that this is the final session. Depending upon your own plans for the group and/or the group views about continuing to meet and study another series, you need to be sensitive to what degree and sense of closure the group needs. Choose one or more of the following options ...*

OPTION 1: *Suggest to the group that redemptive community has had time to take root in your meetings together. Remind them that their healing journeys are only beginning. Ask the group if they would consider staying together for continued support and redemption. Pass around 3 x 5" cards so people can jot down their potential interest. Other related recovery studies in the Picking Up the Pieces series include* Redeeming the Tears *(grief and loss),* Stop the Madness *(addictions) and* Radical Reconciliation *(forgiveness). Consider also* Finding Jesus in the Movies.

OPTION 2: *Encourage group members to join the next* Beyond the Shadows *group, either to go through the process again at a deeper level, or to take to an active role in helping to lead the group as a mentor, small-group facilitator, accountability partner, or some other job that fits well. (As the group facilitator, try to fit people into the most suitable roles).*

OPTION 3: *If there are not enough to form a small group, refer these interested people to your pastor to connect them with an ongoing group. If you form a group that does not want to go through* Beyond the Shadows *again, we suggest your next step would be to go through the Serendipity study entitled* Great Beginnings. *You may order this and other group resources online at www. SerendipityHouse.com.*

OPTION 4: *Some support groups like to meet each month or so for a get-together at a restaurant. You may consider offering that as a recommendation. Knowing that a reunion is not far off may help many group members with this study's wrap-up, especially if you don't plan to continue meeting as a group.*

Taking It Home

LOOKING INWARD: A QUESTION TO TAKE TO MY HEART

✳ What would I be excited or encouraged to see God accomplish by His power through my weakness? Through my current depression?

✻ What do You want to burn into my heart and mind as key truths to hang onto as You empower me in my battle with depression?

NOTE: If the group did not watch the movie *The Legend of Bagger Vance* together, we encourage you to obtain the DVD and watch the entire story. Jot down insights and questions as you watch.

NOTES

_____

_____

_____

_____

_____

_____

_____

_____

_____

_____

_____

_____

_____

_____

_____

_____

REQUIRED SUPPLIES AND PREPARATION
FOR EACH SESSION

This section lists the supplies required for the Group Experiences in each session of the study. The procedural instructions for the experiences are also given within each session.

SESSION 1:

Supplies: - secure a box of 64 Crayola® crayons in advance (for icebreaker option)
- 4" x 6" index cards or blank sheets of paper for each group member

Procedure:

Give each person a 4" x 6" index card or blank sheet of paper. Explain to group members that they're going to participate in a brief writing exercise and will be invited to share their responses with the group. Tell members to imagine placing a "lost" ad in the Lost and Found section of your newspaper. They will describe depressing personal losses in an imaginary ad. Point out the ad examples in the session.

SESSION 2:

Supplies: - 3x5 index cards and pens for each group member
- DVD player and TV
- DVD of the 1993 Harrison Ford movie, *The Fugitive*

Three Truths and a Lie Procedure:

Give each person a 3x5 card or a small sheet of paper and a pen. Read together the following writing instructions included in the session. After allowing a couple of minutes to write, go around the group and ask each person to share his four statements. Then have the group try to guess which of the statements was the lie. Acknowledge the person who is the best at identifying lies. After everyone has a turn, discuss the related questions.

The Truth Will Set You Free Procedure: Have a TV/DVD player set up. Read the introduction in teh session to the group, then play a scene from the film *The Fugitive*, starring Harrison Ford (1993). Show Scene 3, "Trial and Sentencing" (9:40 to 12:58 minutes on the DVD timer). After showing the clip, discuss the questions.

SESSION 3:

Supplies: - Optional: CD *Pursued by God: Redemptive Worship* from SerendipityHouse.com.

Confronting Our Anxieties Procedure:

The primary goal of "Connecting" today is to help group members connect with their own hearts and begin to connect with God. Lead the group in a writing exercise. Be sure to bring pens or pencils to pass around. (*Continued on next page.*)

Confronting Our Anxieties Procedure (continued):

- Allow this experience some time; don't rush it.
- Put on quiet background music (You may purchase the CD *Pursued by God: Redemptive Worship* from Serendipity or select your own music.)
- Help each person create his own personal space. This is not a time to chat; make it very honoring.
- Trust God to speak to each person individually through this exercise.
- After allowing 12-15 minutes to write, invite group members to read their prayers aloud.

SESSION 4:

Supplies: - DVD player and TV
           - DVD of the 2006 film *Miss Potter*

Procedure:

Have a TV/DVD player set up. Read the introduction to the group, and then play the first half of Scene 11 "A Close Friend" from the 2006 film *Miss Potter*, starring Renee Zellweger and Emily Watson. (1:10:05 to 1:14:24 minutes on the DVD timer – up until Miss Potter signs the deed for the country farm). After showing the clip, discuss questions.

SESSION 5:

Supplies: - DVD player and TV
           - DVD of the 2003 Jim Carey film, *Bruce Almighty*
           - DVD of the 2003 film *The Apostle*, starring Robert Duvall

Mighty Complaint Procedure:

Have a TV/DVD player set up. Read the "Mighty Complaint" introduction to the group, and then play Scene 5 "Fired" from the 2003 film *Bruce Almighty* (the scene runs from 17:20 to 23:02 minutes on the DVD timer). After showing the clip, discuss the questions.

So How Do You Really Feel? Procedure:

Use this "Connecting" time to help group members become more real with God. Read aloud the "So How Do You Really Feel?" introduction. Then, show Scene 8, "Yelling at the Lord," from *The Apostle*, where Robert Duvall's character Sonny has a shouting prayer session with God (25:33 to 27:42 minutes on the DVD timer). Discuss the questions.

SESSION 6:

Supplies: - Three small index cards (or sheets of paper) for EACH group member

Tapping in to the Power of Community Procedure:

Have a group member read James 5:16-18 aloud. Then pass out three small index cards to each person. Instruct them to take about 10 minutes on their own to write on each card as indicated. When you pull the group back together, instruct people to pass their card sets to the next person of the same gender on their right.

On Card 1: List a burden, failure, issue, or regret you've been carrying on your own for which you'd appreciate support. Jot it down on the first card, write your name, and give a brief explanation.

On Card 2: List your biggest struggle in dealing with depression for which you'd appreciate support and prayer. Jot it down on the second card, write your name, and give a brief explanation.

On Card 3: What is it that someone could do outside these meetings to be encouraging to you as a friend? Think about the three different types of support we discussed. Jot it down on the third card, write your name, and give a brief explanation.

SESSION 7:

Supplies: - 10-pound (5 kg) dumbbell
- 5-pound (2-2.5 kg) dumbbell

Procedure:
You will need to bring a 10-pound (5 kg) dumbbell to the group. You may want to bring a lighter (5-pound or 2 kg) and a heavier weight, depending on the body types and strength levels of group members. Pass around the weight(s) and invite members to do a few repetitions of bicep curls or overhead presses. Have each group member continue until they feel a strain on their muscles. Then discuss the questions about the Dragon of Resistance.

SESSION 8:

OPTIONAL MOVIE NIGHT: Since *The Legend of Bagger Vance* plays a key role in Session 8, we would encourage you to set up an additional meeting to watch the film together and be prepared to discuss recovering your "authentic swing."

Supplies: - DVD player or Video cassette player
- DVD of the film *The Legend of Bagger Vance*
- 2 Large flat stones marked as indicated in advance

Facing Our Shadows Procedure:
Read the introduction in the session aloud to the group, and then show a scene from the 2000 film, *The Legend of Bagger Vance*, starring Will Smith, Matt Damon, and Charlize Theron. Show part of Chapter 29 "The Drop" (begin about 4 minutes in at 1:37:08 and continue to end of Chapter 29 at 1:43:35 on the DVD timer). After showing the clip, discuss the following questions.

Full Life in a Troubled World Procedure:
Write "*Life ... Joy ... Peace. John 10:10*" on one large flat stone.
Write "*Trouble ... Pain ... Sorrow. John 16:33*" on another to illustrate the idea that we must accept both joy/peace and pain/suffering coexisting in this life. Pass the stones around the group so each member holds them. You might want to create a set of stones for each group member to take home as a reminder.

Leading a Successful Recovery Group

You need to accept the limitations of leadership. You cannot transform a life. You must lead your group to the Bible, the Holy Spirit, and the power of Christian community. By doing so your group will have all the tools necessary to walk through the healing journey and embrace life and hope on the other side. The journey must extend well beyond this study. But the experience will allow your group members to move toward wholeness.

Make the following things available at each session
- *Beyond the Shadows* book for each attendee
- Bible for each attendee
- Boxes of tissue
- Snacks and refreshments plus dark chocolates (calming properties)
- Pens or pencils for each attendee

NOTE: Every session requires other supplies for the group experiences that greatly enhance the healing journey. Check the supplies list and be sure you gather what's needed in each session.

The Setting

General Tips:

1. Prepare for each meeting by reviewing the material, praying for each group member, asking the Holy Spirit to join you, and making Jesus the centerpiece of every experience.

2. Create the right environment by making sure chairs are arranged so each person can see the eyes of every other attendee. Set the room temperature at 69 degrees. If meeting in a home, make sure pets are in a location where they cannot interrupt the meeting. Request that cell phones are turned off unless someone is expecting an emergency call. Have music playing as people arrive (volume low enough for people to converse) and, if possible, burn a sweet-smelling candle.

3. Try to have soft drinks and coffee available for early arrivals.

4. Have someone with the spiritual gift of hospitality ready to make any new attendees feel welcome.

5. Be sure there is adequate lighting so that everyone can read without straining.

6. There are four types of questions used in each session: Observation (What is the passage telling us?), Interpretation (What does the passage mean?), Self-revelation (How am I doing in light of the truth unveiled?), and Application (Now that I know what I know, what will I do to integrate this truth into my life?). You may not have time to use all the questions in each session, but be sure to use some from each of these types of questions.

7. Connect with group members away from group time. The amount of participation you'll receive from group member during meetings is directly related to the amount of time that you connect with them away from the meetings.

8. Don't get impatient about the depth of relationship group members are experiencing. Building real Christian Community takes time.

9. Be sure pens and/or pencils are available for attendees at each meeting.

10. Never ask someone to pray aloud without first getting their permission. Ask for volunteers to help with various aspects of the group, including reading aloud.

EVERY MEETING:

1. Before the icebreakers, do not say, "Now we're going to do an icebreaker." The meeting should feel like a conversation from beginning to end, not a classroom experience.

2. Be certain every member responds to the icebreaker questions. The goal is for every person to hear his own voice early in the meeting. People will then feel comfortable to converse later on. If group members can't think of a response, let them know you'll come back to them after the others have spoken.

3. Remember, a great group leader talks less than 10% of the time. If you ask a question and no one answers, just wait. If you create an environment where you fill the gaps of silence, the group will quickly learn they needn't join you in the conversation.

4. Don't be hesitant to call people by name as you ask them to respond to questions or to give their opinions. Be sensitive, but engage everyone in the conversation.

5. Don't ask people to read aloud unless you have gotten their permission prior to the meeting. Feel free to ask for volunteers to read.

THE GROUP

Every group is made up of a unique set of personalities, backgrounds, and life experiences. This diversity creates a dynamic distinctivefor each group. Embracing the unique character of your group and its individuals is vital to a deep healing experience.

Treat each person as special, responsible, and valuable members of this Christian community. By doing so you'll bring out the best in each of them thus creating a living, breathing, life-changing group dynamic.

WHAT CAN YOU EXPECT?

Because group members are still experiencing and emotions are stirring within them, at the outset, members will be on their best behavior. Some attendees will, as they understand the openness necessary and requested by the group, withdraw for at time.

Some attendees will experience fatigue which will lead to them shutting down emotionally. This is natural and is one of the things our body does to prevent overload.

There are emotions and phases unique to people dealing with depression and anxiety. These will be addressed as the group progresses through the healing journey. Be sensitive.

You will be the most helpful when you focus on how each individual is adjusting and reminding them that hurt, anger , and other emotions are normal and extremely helpful to understand and express on the path to healing..

If there's severe depression, or short tempers, changes in physical habits, such as sleep, eating, apathy, and others appear to be long term, refer people to a pastor or competent Christian counselor. **You can get a list of counselors from your pastor or www.aacc.net.**

Places may also bring back memories or temptations that are difficult to deal with alone. If a member has an engagement in a location that would be a painful reminder of the past go with them and/or ask the group members if one of them might be there for this individual. You may hear, "This is something I have to do alone." You can respect this desire, but remind them that it's God who will give them strength, and that you will pray.

WHAT CAN YOU DO?

Support – Provide plenty of time for support among the group members. Encourage members to connect with each other between meetings. It's very important that you help each person in the group to develop a strong, supportive accountability group

Shared Feelings – Reassure the members how normal their feelings are; even if relief and sadness are mixed together. Encourage the members to share their feelings with one another.

Advice Giving – Encourage cross-talk (members talking to each other), but limit advice giving. "Should" and "ought to" statements tend to increase the guilt and shame.

Silence – Silence is not a problem. Even though it may seem awkward, silence is just a sign that people are not ready to talk. It DOES NOT mean they aren't thinking or feeling. If the silence needs to be broken, be sure you break it with the desire to move forward.

Prayer – Prayer is vital to healing. Starting and ending with prayer is important. However, people may need prayer in the middle of the session. If a member is sharing and you sense a need to pray, then begin to look for a place to add it.

Feelings vs. Right Choices and Thinking – There may be a temptation to overemphasize feelings rather that choices and thinking. It is important that you encourage the group to keep moving forward regardless of how we feel. Processing emotions is a vital aspect of the healing journey, but left to feelings alone, progress will shut down.

As you move toward the end of the study, be aware that it is a bittersweet time for the group. It will be painful for them to say goodbye to one another. Set a time for the group to have a reunion.

GROUP MEETING STRUCTURE

Each of your group meetings will include a four-part agenda.

1. BREAKING THE ICE:

This section includes fun, uplifting questions to warm up the group and help group members get to know one another better, as they begin the journey of becoming a connected community. These questions prepare the group for meaningful discussion throughout the session.

2. DISCOVERING THE TRUTH:

The heart of each session is the interactive Bible study time. The goal is for the group to discover biblical truths through open, discovery questions that lead to further investigation. The emphasis in this section is two-fold:
(1) to provide instruction about the process of recovery and freedom; and
(2) understand what the Bible says through interaction within your group.

NOTE: To help the group experience a greater sense of community, it is important for everybody to participate in the "Discovering the Truth" and "Embracing the Truth" discussions. Even though people in a group have differing levels of biblical knowledge, it is vital that group members encourage one another share what they are observing, thinking, and feeling about the Bible passages.

3. EMBRACING THE TRUTH:

All study should direct group members to action and life change. This section continues the Bible study time, but with an emphasis on leading group members toward integrating the truths they have discovered into their lives. The questions are very practical and application-focused.

4. CONNECTING:

One of the key goals of this study is to lead group members to grow closer to one another as the group develops a sense of community. This section focuses on further application, as well as opportunities for encouraging, supporting, and praying for one another.

TAKING IT HOME:

Between each session, there is some homework for group members. This includes a question to take to God or a question to take to the heart, and typically a few questions to help prepare for the next session. These experiences are a critical part of your journey of healing and freedom.